So you really want to learn

French

Book Three
Answer Book

Nigel Pearce B.A. M.C.I.L.

Editor: Joyce Capek

GALORE PARK

www.galorepark.co.uk

Published by Galore Park Publishing,
19/21 Sayers Lane, Tenterden, Kent TN30 6BW
www.galorepark.co.uk

Text copyright © Nigel Pearce 2007
Illustrations copyright Galore Park 2007

The right of Nigel Pearce to be identified as the author of this Work has been
asserted by him in accordance with sections 77 and 78 of the Copyright,
Designs and Patents Act 1988.

Typography Typetechnique, London W1
Illustrations by Ian Douglass

Printed by CPI Antony Rowe, Chippenham

ISBN-13: 978 1902984 90 2

First published 2007

Details of other Galore Park publications are available at
www.galorepark.co.uk

ISEB Revision Guides, publications and examination papers may also be
obtained from Galore Park.

Contents

Preface

Welcome to *So you really want to learn French Book Three Answers*. Included are full transcripts of the readings on Audio CD which is available to accompany this course (ISBN 9781902984919). These answers are not intended to be prescriptive but should provide guidance to those using the course.

Chapitre 1

Back to School

Exercice 1.1

It's September. The leaves have begun to change colour and some have already fallen from the trees. However, it's still nice and warm. There's no wind, but the sun has lost its strength and you can feel winter coming. It's time to go back to school. Georges and Martine have just returned home after long holidays at the seaside. They've enjoyed themselves, but they've rested too. The children have discovered many interesting things. They've finally found the name of the mysterious «J-P.L.», the owner of the silver box that their neighbour, Mr Simonneau, has found in his garden. Martine was nevertheless looking forward to seeing her friends again on going back to school.

Exercice 1.2

Martine.	Sabine! How are you? Have you had a good holiday?
Sabine.	You bet! We went to the USA. It was brilliant!
Martine.	Where exactly did you go?
Sabine.	First to Virginia, then to Texas, passing through Louisiana.
Martine.	You visited New Orleans?
Sabine.	Oh yes. What's more, my father is a jazz fan.
Martine.	Great! We went to Tunisia.
Sabine.	The weather must have been good there. You are really tanned.
Martine.	You can tell, can't you?
Sabine.	Which class are you in this year?
Martine.	The same as yours! Haven't you looked at the lists?
Sabine.	No. I've only just got here.

1. L'histoire se passe en automne.

2. Il fait beau et (assez) chaud.

3. La Nouvelle Orléans est en Louisiane, aux Etats-Unis.

4. Ils ont découvert le nom du mystérieux «J-P. L.».

5. M. Simonneau est le voisin de Martine et Georges.

Exercice 1.3

1. My sister (has) dropped the vase which my mother bought this morning.

2. Paul's neighbour had a tummy ache; she sent for the doctor.

3. Why don't you make a greenhouse?

4. Little Thierry wanted to play football. I let him do it.

5. Martine dropped the jug of water that she was carrying.

Exercice 1.4

1. On est au mois de septembre.

2. Quelques-unes sont déjà tombées.

3. Georges et Martine viennent de rentrer.

4. Ils se sont amusés.

5. Le propriétaire de la boîte.

6. En rentrant au collège.

7. On est allés aux Etats-Unis.

8. En passant par la Louisiane.

9. Mon père est fanatique de jazz.

10. Tu es dans quelle classe?

Exercice 1.5

1. On était au mois de septembre.

2. Quelques-uns sont déjà partis.

3. Jean et Sabine viennent de téléphoner.

4. On va s'amuser.

5. Le propriétaire du vélo.

6. En trouvant le livre.

7. Elle est allée en France.

8. En passant par le pont.

9. Ma mère est fanatique de musique.

10. Il est dans quelle pièce?

11. Quelques-unes des filles sont sorties.

12. On était au mois de juin et il faisait (très) beau.

13. En passant par la porte, elle est tombée.

14. Georges ne s'est pas amusé au bord de la mer.

15. Il était dans quelle voiture quand ils se sont arrêtés.

Exercice 1.6

Georges.	Hey! Tochiko! How are things?
Tochiko.	Fine! What about you?
Georges.	OK. I don't know where to go.
Tochiko.	Haven't you looked?
Georges.	Not yet. Where are the form lists?
Tochiko.	They are posted in the corridor, next to the lockers.
Georges.	Thanks. Are you coming to the party?
Tochiko.	What party?
Georges.	This evening at half-past seven. At our house. It's to celebrate Martine's birthday.
Tochiko.	I don't think so.
Georges.	Why?
Tochiko.	Euh … I have to ask Mum …

1. Il ne sait pas où aller parce qu'il n'a pas regardé les listes des classes.

2. A côté des casiers, il y a les listes des classes.

3. C'est ce soir.

4. Tochiko ne peut pas venir à la boum.

5. Elle dit qu'elle doit demander à sa maman.

Exercice 1.7

Hi Mina,

I'm at school. It's OK, but everything's new. I'm in 6M with Mrs Meunier. She's quite nice but she's a Geography teacher and I find it difficult. I have a problem. I've been invited to a party this evening for Martine's birthday, but I don't want to go to it because they've given us heaps of homework and I want to work this year. I really need to find an excuse! Help me! Answer quickly!

Love,

Toch'

Pupils are required to insert the correct words from the box into the spaces. There are more words than necessary in the box, so that pupils may identify the correct ones (marked in bold).

Tochiko … **était** … à l'école … **quand** … elle a … **envoyé** … un e-mail à Mina. Elle … **aime** … Madame Meunier, mais elle n'aime pas … **beaucoup** … la géographie. Elle … **la** … trouve difficile. Tochiko voulait … **faire** … ses … **devoirs** …, donc elle … **a** … demandé à Mina de … **trouver** … une excuse.

Exercice 1.8

Here is a possible response from Mina, using the phrases suggested:

Salut Toch'

Quelle horreur! Tu pourrais dire que le chat est malade … ou bien dis-lui que tu es très fatiguée. Mais tu pourrais dire la vérité!!

Bon courage,

Mina

Hi Toch'

How ghastly! You could say that the cat's ill ... or tell her that you are really tired. But you could always tell the truth!!

Good luck,

Mina

Exercice 1.9

Pair work.

Pupils make up a dialogue in which they have to give an excuse for not going out. For example:

A. Hello?

B. Hi Paul. It's me, Jacques. Do you want to go to the cinema tonight?

A. Sorry, I can't. I …

Here are a few suggestions:

… maman m'a dit que je dois faire mes devoirs de maths.

… je ne peux pas sortir – je suis malade.

… j'ai promis d'aider papa avec l'ordinateur.

… ma grand-mère va venir nous voir.

Exercice 1.10

At school, there is an international correspondence club organised by a teacher. Martine has an English pen-friend, Peter, but Tochiko and Philippe don't. Philippe looks at the ads in the club newsletter. Philippe likes to go to discos, walking in the mountains, playing basketball, listening to rap music on the radio and cycling. Tochiko loves classical music, going to the beach, eating oriental food, and reading crime novels.

Pupils have to choose ideal pen-friends for Philippe and Tochiko from the adverts, and give reasons for their choices.

International Correspondence Club		
First name	**Joshua**	**Mireille**
Nationality	English	Swiss
Age	13	12
Likes	football	dancing
	sports cars	sport
	Mozart	cycling
Dislikes	the countryside	ancient music

First name	**Claudia**	**Mark**
Nationality	German	American
Age	12	13
Likes	walks	Japanese cooking
	jazz	19th century music
	reading	reading
Dislikes	sport	comic books

Ideal correspondents:

Philippe: **Mireille**: she likes dancing and cycling, and doesn't like ancient music.

Tochiko: **Mark**: he likes eastern food and classical music.

Exercice 1.11

Pupils produce a 'small ad' for themselves, set out as in Exercise 1.10:

First name	
Nationality	
Age	
Likes	
Dislikes	

"A question for the curious among you:"

Answer: because the word nationalité is feminine.

Exercice 1.12

1.   C'est moi **qui** ai écrit la lettre.

2.   **Qui** est dans ma classe cette année?

3.   Tochiko n'aime pas les enfants **qui** se plaignent tout le temps.

4.   **Qui** a lu le nouveau Harry Potter?

5.   C'est un bouquin **que** tout le monde aime énormément.

6.   **Qui** est le Président de la République?

7.   **Que** va-t-on manger ce soir?

8.   On va manger les escalopes **que** tu as choisies hier.

9.   Le disque **que** tu écoutes est le mien.

10.   C'est ma mère **qui** va faire la cuisine.

11.   Où sont les cahiers **qu'** elle cherche?

12.   Le livre **qu'** il veut lire est excellent.

13.   Les repas **qu'** on sert au collège sont assez bons.

14.   Le prof **qui** parle en ce moment s'appelle M. Béchet.

15.   Où as-tu mis le magazine **que** je veux lire?

Exercice 1.13

| 1. | **qui** | **pronom interrogatif** |

2.   que   pronom relatif

3.   que   conjonction

4.   qu'   pronom relatif

5.   qu'   conjonction

6.   que   pronom interrogatif

7.   qu'   pronom relatif

Exercice 1.14

Who likes history? Do you like it? So do I. The subjects that I have to do at school are all very interesting. I know that my friends are going out this evening, but the cinema that they like is closed. It's true that you can find other cinemas, but what are you going to do if you don't like the films that they show there?

Exercice 1.15

Model answer

Salut Joséphine,

Comment vas-tu? Moi, ça va, mais je viens de rentrer au collège! Ce matin je suis allé(e) à l'école en bus pour la première fois. Je suis arrivé(e) ici à huit heures. Il y a beaucoup de garçons et de filles. Je suis dans la classe de Mme Meunier. J'ai un nouvel ami: il s'appelle Bernard et il aime les chevaux, comme moi. A midi, on a mangé du steak hâché-frites à la cantine. C'était assez bon mais je préfère la nourriture à la maison!

Cette année je vais faire français, anglais, maths, histoire-géo, allemand et sciences-nat.

A plus

(...)

Exercice 1.16

It's afternoon at school. Martine, Georges, Tochiko and Philippe are outside, in the playground.

Martine.	What do you have this afternoon?
Philippe.	I've got an hour of English and a Spanish lesson.
Tochiko.	I love Spanish. It's a lovely language, and it's useful. Me, I've got History-Geography and Biology.
Philippe.	What have *you* got, Georges?
Georges.	I don't know, I haven't looked!
Tochiko.	Right, who's had a nice lunch?
Philippe.	Me! I had pasta with Neopolitan sauce.
Martine.	You did right. I had a *salade niçoise* and tomatoes. It wasn't very good.
Tochiko.	I had salad as well, but I had grated cheese with it.
Martine.	You did? Was there cheese? I didn't see it!
Georges.	*(Looks at his timetable)* Ah. I've Maths and Biology.
Martine.	Tochiko, is it true that you can't come to my party?
Tochiko.	Yes it's true. I'm sorry, Martine, but I promised Mum I'd work hard this year, and I've got two hours of homework to do for tomorrow.
Martine.	Don't worry, it doesn't matter. I understand.

1. She has History-Geography and Biology

2. She likes Spanish and thinks it is useful.

3. Georges hasn't looked yet to see which lessons he has.

4. She says she has promised her Mum that she will work hard this year, and she has two hours of homework to do for tomorrow.

5. Martine quite understands and tells her not to worry.

Exercice 1.17

Back to school

You are at school in France with a French friend.

Pupil (you)	Examiner (teacher or partner)
1. Le cours finit à quelle heure?	
	A 12 h 30.
2. J'ai faim!	
	On va manger dans une demi-heure.
3. Il y a des devoirs?	
	Pour moi, oui. Pas pour toi!
	Tu aimes l'histoire?
4. Oui, je l'aime bien.	

Exercice 1.18

In the school canteen

You are in the school canteen with a French friend.

Pupil	Examiner
1. La cantine est énorme!	
	Oui, c'est vrai.
2. Où est-ce que je peux m'asseoir?	
	Mets-toi à côté de moi.
3. La nourriture est délicieuse.	
	Oui.
	Mais tu n'aimes pas le poisson?
4. Non. Je préfère la viande.	

Exercice 1.19

In the evening at the French penfriend's home

You are in the sitting room with the family. You are talking to the father.

Pupil	Examiner
1. J'aime l'école de Philippe.	
	Oui, nous avons de la chance.
2. Est-ce qu'il y a des ordinateurs?	
	Bien sûr! Tu aimes l'informatique?

3. Ah oui.
   J'ai un nouvel ordinateur à la maison.

4. Le dîner est à quelle heure?

   D'habitude on mange à 20 heures.

Exercice 1.20

In this exercise, pupils have to prepare to say in French a few things about their life and work at school. The suggestions in brackets show where substitutions might be made by the pupil:

D'habitude j'arrive en classe à (huit heures et quart).
   Usually I get to school at (8.15)

Dans ma classe, nous sommes (dix-sept).
   In my form there are (17) of us.

Le matin, avant le déjeuner, on a (cinq) cours.
   In the morning, before lunch, we have (5) lessons.

On mange (bien) à la cantine.
   We eat (well) in the school dining room.

Aujourd'hui, on est (jeudi). J'aime les (jeudis) mais je préfère les (lundis) parce que nous avons (latin) et j'adore ça.
   Today it's (Thursday). I like (Thursdays) but I prefer (Mondays) because we have (Latin) and I love that.

Aujourd'hui on a (anglais) et je ne l'aime pas beaucoup parce que (le prof est sévère).
   Today we have (English) and I don't like it much because (the teacher is strict).

Les classes finissent à (dix-sept heures) et je rentre (à la maison) (en bus).
   Lessons finish at (5.00 pm) and I go home (by bus).

Exercice 1.21

Pupils write an index prompt-card like the example given:

arrival 8.15	
class, classroom	
friends, m. and f.	
lessons	
school food	
Monday – sport	
English – teacher	
lessons	
home	

Exercice 1.22

Dictée

CD
9

J'ai reçu une lettre // de ma cousine. // Elle m'a raconté // sa visite aux Etats-Unis. // Quand elle est revenue, // elle a téléphoné // immédiatement // à sa mère.

Vive la France!

Etre et avoir

(a) *Etre et avoir* is a very unusual French film, which had enormous and unexpected success. It's the story of a school in the Auvergne region of central southern France in which all the pupils are in one single class. The teacher, Mr Lopez, has to teach the children everything they need to know, from kindergarten to the end of primary school: that is to say from the age of 5 to 11 years. There are no actors in this film, for, when they began to film it, they were only going to do a documentary on one of the few remaining schools of this type in France, but the total lack of any commentary gave it an air of authenticity and the film was soon hailed as a masterpiece. We see everything: the snow falling in winter while the municipal minibus does the rounds of the houses and farms to bring the children to school, family problems and the private lives of the pupils, the long walks and the picnics …

(b) 1. Dans cette école, il y a deux grandes classes.   Faux
          Dans cette école, il y a **une** grande classe.
          *In this school, there is **one** large class.*

     2. Il n'y a pas d'acteurs dans le film.   Vrai

     3. Le professeur s'appelle Monsieur Lopez.   Vrai

     4. Il y a beaucoup d'écoles comme celle-ci en France.   Faux
          Cette école est une des dernières de ce genre.
          This school is one of the last of this type.

     5. Il n'y a pas de commentaire pendant le film.   Vrai

(c) 1. Il y a un … **minibus** … pour amener les enfants à l'école.

     2. Monsieur Lopez connaît bien les familles de ses … **élèves** …

     3. On … **peut** … aller à cette école dès l'âge de cinq ans.

     4. Au début, ce film allait être un … **documentaire** …

     5. En été, l'instituteur fait des … **promenades** … avec ses élèves.

Chapitre 2

Everyday life – work and leisure

Exercice 2.1

(CD 10)

At Georges and Martine's house, it's not just 'back to school, it's 'back to work' for the parents. The children went back to school a week ago, and Dad has also had to get up early to be at his office on time! The children have changed forms, and Dad has changed offices. On 1st September he became a Head of Department. Mum has just found a job, too: she's employed at the post office. Their neighbour Mr Simonneau is lucky. He's retired. He can get up when he wants to, but every morning, when he leaves home at 7.30, Dad sees him already out in his garden or his greenhouse.

Dad.	Morning, Paul!
Mr. Simonneau.	Good morning!
Dad.	You get up early!
Mr Simonneau.	Oh yes. When the weather's fine I always get up at about seven.
Dad.	Seven o'clock! Don't you like sleeping?
Mr Simonneau.	Of course I do! It's just that I go to bed early. There's never anything interesting on TV. I have dinner at eight then I read the paper or write some articles, or letters.
Dad.	Articles?
Mr Simonneau.	Yes. I'm president of the village horticultural society, so I have to produce a monthly newsletter.
Dad.	You give yourself a lot of work!
Mr Simonneau.	Not really, it's a pleasure. I do it for fun! What do you do at the weekend? Do you have a lie-in? We don't see you in the garden very often before lunchtime!
Dad.	No! It's true that I get up a little later, but I'm the one who makes breakfast for the whole family at the weekend. I go downstairs with Georges. It's the ladies who stay in bed! Georges goes to get the bread and the croissants, and we sit down to eat at nine o'clock. Oh no! It's nearly eight! Off to work! Cheers Paul!
Mr Simonneau.	Cheerio! Have a nice day!
Dad.	Thanks!

1.   They went back to school a week ago.

2.   He has been promoted: he's now a Department Head.

3.   He can please himself because he is retired.

4.   He gets up at seven when the weather is fine.

5.   He can get up early because he goes to bed early.

6.   He sometimes writes letters or articles.

7.   He thinks there is never anything good on TV.

8.   He must produce a monthly review.

9.   He is not seen in the garden because he makes the breakfast for the whole family.

10. Georges goes to get the bread and croissants.

Exercice 2.2

1.   Je me couche toujours de bonne heure.

2.   Rien d'intéressant.

3.   Ou bien j'écris des articles.

4.   Je suis obligé de …

5.   Je le fais pour m'amuser.

6.   C'est moi qui …

7.   On se met à table.

8.   Presque huit heures.

9.   Au boulot.

10. Bonne journée.

Exercice 2.3

1.   Maman se couche toujours tard.

2.   Quelque chose d'intéressant.

3.   Ou bien je promène le chien.

4.   Elle était obligée de …

5.   On le fait pour s'amuser.

6.   C'est moi qui range ma chambre.

7.   Il se met à table.

8.   Presque midi. / Presque l'heure déjeuner.

9.   Bonne soirée!

10.   Bon weekend!

11.   C'est nous qui écrivons des articles.

12.   Elles l'ont fait pour s'amuser.

13.   Je vais me mettre à table.

14.   Ils vont être obligés de partir.

15.   Quelque chose d'épatant. / Quelque chose d'incroyable.

Exercice 2.4

Dictée

Les enfants // sont rentrés à la maison // après une longue journée // à l'école. // Maman leur a donné // des pains au chocolat.

Exercice 2.5

At school, the lessons finish at 17.30, that is to say 5.30 pm. There is a bus at 5.45 so, instead of going straight home, Georges chats with a few friends in the covered courtyard and Martine spends her time flicking through a magazine. When they arrive home, Martine takes the key from her school bag and opens the front door. No-one is there because Mum comes home at 6.30 and Dad usually arrives shortly afterwards. So it's Georges who feeds the cat and Martine who lays the table for the evening meal. The cat is very happy to see the young people again. He purrs with pleasure while eating his dinner. Georges knows that he loves milk, and pours a little for him in a saucer.

Vrai ou faux?

1. A l'école, les classes se terminent avant seize heures.   Faux
   Les classes se terminent **après** seize heures.
   *Lessons finish **after** 4 pm.*

2. Après les classes, Georges et Martine retournent immédiatement
   à la maison.   Faux
   Les enfants rentrent **plus tard** à la maison.
   *The children go home **later**.*

3. Georges parle avec ses copains pendant que Martine lit.   Vrai

4. Maman ouvre la porte quand les enfants arrivent.   Faux
   C'est **Martine** qui ouvre la porte.
   ***Martine** opens the door.*

5. Papa rentre à la maison avant maman.   Faux
   Maman rentre à la maison avant **Papa**.
   Mum** gets home before **Dad.

6. Le soir à la maison, le frère de Martine s'occupe du chat.   Vrai

7. Le chat mange son dîner en même temps que la famille.   Faux
   Le chat mange son dîner **avant** la famille.
   *The cat has his dinner **before** the family.*

8. Le chat aime son dîner.   Vrai

Exercice 2.6

In the evening, at home.

Georges.	What's the time?
Martine.	I don't know. I didn't put my watch on. Look at the sitting-room clock.
Georges.	Sh! Listen! Did you hear that? Dad's home.
Martine.	I'll have a look. No. It's Mum ...
Georges.	I'll open the door for her. (I'll let her in).

***

Mum.	Phew! What a day!
Martine.	Hi, Mum. So you've had a hard day?
Mum.	Absolutely.

Georges.	But you go around the village putting letters in letter-boxes. That's not difficult!
Martine.	Don't worry, Mum, he doesn't understand!
Georges.	What don't I understand?
Mum.	Firstly, that I don't post letters in boxes! Today I worked at the counter and I had lots of difficult customers! And then the electric weighing scales broke!
Martine.	Shall I give you a hand with the supper, Mum?
Mum.	Yes, please. Will you prepare the vegetables and wash the salad? I'm going to change.
Martine.	Sure. What are we eating?
Mum.	Whiting fillets and melon. I bought it yesterday at the market.

Exercice 2.7

1. She hasn't put her watch on.

2. She tells him to go and look at the clock in the sitting room.

3. He thinks she has been delivering letters.

4. She was working in the post office at the counter.

5. She had had some difficult customers.

6. The electric scales stopped working.

7. She asks her to prepare the vegetables and wash the salad.

8. She will be changing.

9. She bought it in the market the day before.

Exercice 2.8

1. Il est quelle heure?

2. La pendule du salon.

3. Tu as entendu ça?

4. C'est papa qui rentre.

5. Je vais lui ouvrir.

6. Quelle journée!

7.   Tu fais le tour du village.

8.   Je te donne un coup de main avec le dîner?

9.   Je vais me changer.

10.   Je l'ai acheté.

Exercice 2.9

1.   La pendule de la cuisine.

2.   La table de la salle à manger.

3.   Tu as vu ça?

4.   C'est Marie qui sort.

5.   Tu vas m'ouvrir.

6.   Quelle belle robe!

7.   Ils font le tour de la ville.

8.   Je donne un coup de main à papa?

9.   Elle va se changer.

10.   Elle l'a acheté.

11.   Le toit de la remise.

12.   Ils ont réparé ça?

13.   Le bruit? C'était Jean et Philippe qui travaillaient dans le garage.

14.   Quel vieux bâtiment!

15.   C'est l'appartement de la soeur de ma mère.

Exercice 2.10

1.   Je n'ai pas regardé la pendule.

2.   La pendule n'était pas sur la cheminée.

3.   Elle n'a pas vu maman.

4.   Marie ne sort pas tous les soirs.

5.   Elle ne va pas ouvrir la porte.

6.   Ce n'est pas une belle maison.

7.   Pierre ne veut pas goûter le fromage de chèvre.

8.   Claire ne donne pas souvent un coup de main à maman dans la cuisine.

9.   Vous n'allez pas vous changer?

10. Paul ne peut pas les acheter.

11. Ce n'était pas moi qui réparais la remise.

12. Maman n'a pas emménagé au mois de décembre.

13. L'appartement n'était pas propre.

14. Je ne pouvais pas tout voir de la fenêtre.

15. Il n'y avait pas de balcon.

Exercice 2.11

This is a five minute timed speaking exercise. After writing rough notes in French, pupils should then deliver the 'situation' – all within 5 minutes.

Suggested presentations:

1.   J'arrive à la maison à 17 h 50. Il n'y a personne. J'ouvre la porte et je rentre. Papa rentre juste après moi, puis c'est Jérôme qui arrive. Je commence à préparer le repas du soir.

2.   Je suis arrivé(e) à la maison à 17 h 50. Il n'y avait personne. J'ai ouvert la porte et je suis rentré(e). Papa est rentré juste après moi, puis c'est Jérôme qui est arrivé. J'ai commencé à préparer le repas du soir.

Exercice 2.12

Household chores

One day, at school, all the pupils are speaking in front of the class about household tasks, that is to say, the little jobs they have to do to help their parents at home. Georges's and Martine's parents both work, so everyone is obliged to help out. Last week, for example, Martine helped a lot in the kitchen and Georges worked in the garden. They were asked what they did.

Teacher.   Georges, what did you do last week, to help your parents?

Georges.   Well, I worked in the garden. I mowed the lawn, which is quite hard at the moment because the mower is quite old and can break down from one moment to the next! Then Dad asked me to plant some bulbs on the edge of the terrace. He said that they were going to produce tulips in the spring. After that, I had to dig holes to put garlic bulbs in. To dig, I used a spade. I prepared the ground for vegetables with a fork, I tore up the weeds and I raked everything with a rake after having planted the seeds with a trowel. Then I watered them, of course.

Teacher.   Thank you, Georges, It's easy to see you like gardening!

Georges.   Oh yes, I really do like it.

Teacher.   What about you, Martine? What did you do?

Martine.   As for me, I helped mostly in the kitchen, because we usually get home before Mum and Dad. Last week, I laid the table every evening, and on Monday I helped to get the meal ready. First I had to peel the potatoes. I had to put them in a big saucepan, then I added water and salt. It makes a noise when you turn on the tap to make the cold water flow, and then you have a job turning it off! I lit the gas and I put the pan on the cooker. After the meal, Georges cleared the table but it was Mum who put everything away in the cupboards.

Teacher.   And do you do anything else, to help at home?

Martine.   Yes. I clean the car. I love to make the bodywork shine!

Numbered vocabulary exercise.

1.	creuser	to dig
2.	le trou	hole
3.	arracher	to tear up, to pull up
4.	le râteau	rake
5.	la graine	seed
6.	arroser	to water
7.	éplucher	to peel
8.	ajouter	to add
9.	fermer un robinet	to turn off a tap
10.	couler	to flow

Exercice 2.13
All the vocabulary in **Exercice 2.12** is to be learnt, and tested by the teacher.

Exercice 2.14
Salut Tochiko,

Ça fait une heure et demie que je … **suis** … dans ma chambre. Je … **m'** … ennuie, parce que j' … **ai** … fini mes … **devoirs** … et je … **n'** … ai pas de bon livre à … **lire** … Il pleut, et je … **déteste** … le mauvais **temps** … Hier, j'ai … **dû** … aider mon père dans la … **cuisine** … On a … **mangé** … des filets de … **poisson** … et de la salade. Je n'aime pas faire la cuisine, je … **préfère** … travailler … **dans** … le jardin mais c'est … **mon** … frère Jules qui … **fait** … ça.

Exercice 2.15
Translation of email

Hi Stéphane,

So, you have to work at home too! I don't mind. I have to help Dad with the gardening but I like that. Yes, on Sundays, I do chores around the house: I clear the table, and I take the bins out. No, I don't get bored. I receive ten euros a week.

Here, today, it's nice. Yesterday, like where you were, it was cold.

No, in the evenings, I do my homework in my room, not in front of the television – I have trouble concentrating.

My parents are fine, thank you. I hope you can repair your bike. Yes, I love cycling.

See you soon,

Georges

The following is a model answer for the email which Georges might have received.

Essential information and questions, which should be expressed somewhere in the pupil's answer, are in bold in the pupil's book.

Salut Georges,

Je suis fatigué. C'est dimanche, mais je dois travailler! Je n'aime pas ça. Et toi? Qu'est-ce que tu fais pour aider tes parents? Tu t'ennuies? Est-ce que tes parents te donnent de l'argent? Combien?

Quel temps fait-il chez toi? Ici il fait froid.

J'aime regarder la télévision quand je fais mes devoirs.

Et toi? Comment vont tes parents? Demain je vais aller à l'école à pied – mon vélo est tombé en panne. Tu aimes le cyclisme?

Exercice 2.16

CD
14

A telephone conversation.

Mina.	Ciao Tochiko!
Tochiko.	So now you speak Italian?
Mina.	Yes – one word! Anyway, why did you call me?
Tochiko.	Where are you?
Mina.	In the garden. Why?
Tochiko.	What are you going to do on Saturday?
Mina.	Same as you. We're going to clean the garage. Remember?
Tochiko.	Oh yes. So we can't go to the concert.
Mina.	Which concert?
Tochiko.	The open-air Danny Lefou concert in La Roche …
Mina.	Danny Lefou!!
Tochiko.	Yes, but the garage …

Mina.	Why didn't you tell me? Danny in La Roche! … What time does it start?
Tochiko.	Half-past twelve.
Mina.	We can do the cleaning afterwards!
Tochiko.	I have already bought tickets.
Mina.	I hate you.
Tochiko.	Thanks. See you this evening, little sister.

Exercice 2.17

Pupils must change the details (names, places, chores, pop star's name, the town, the gender-based words such as 'sister') then prepare and perform the phone conversation in pairs.

Exercice 2.18

1. J'aime porter des vêtements chics, mais ils sont chers.   **Marc**
   I like to wear fashionable clothes but they are expensive.

2. Je ne fais pas beaucoup mais mes parents me donnent assez d'argent.
   I don't do much but my parents give me enough money.   **Françoise**

3. Ma mère n'a pas le temps de travailler dans le jardin.   **Luc**
   My mother does not have the time to work in the garden.

4. Je suis très content parce que mon père a les mêmes intérêts
   que moi.
   I am very happy because my father has the same interests as me.   **Jean-Paul**

5. Ma copine reçoit quarante euros par semaine.
   My friend receives forty euros a week.   **Sandrine**

6. Un jour par semaine je rentre de l'école à midi.   **Luc**
   One day a week I come home from school at lunchtime.

7. Je mets les couteaux et les bols sur la table pour toute la famille.
   I put the knives and bowls on the table for the whole family.   **Françoise**

8. Mon père n'habite pas avec nous.   **Luc**
   My father does not live with us.

9. Nous avons trois chats et c'est moi qui leur donne à manger.   **Jean-Paul**
    We have three cats and it's my job to feed them.

10. J'ai voulu acheter un beau jean mais ma mère a dit que
    c'était beaucoup trop cher.   **Marc**
    *I wanted to buy a nice pair of jeans but my mother said they were
    much too expensive.*

Exercice 2.19

1. Notre table est bleue, mais celle de Paul est rouge.

2. Le père de Sandrine est italien, mais celui de Martine est français.

3. Mon T-shirt est vert comme celui de Pierre.

4. Le chien de Charles est bruyant, mais celui de Sophie est calme.

5. Ton journal est intéressant; celui de papa est ennuyeux!

6. Mon stylo est noir, mais celui (qui est) sur la table est gris.

7. Sa serviette est blanche, mais celle de sa soeur est bleue.

8. Notre voiture est une Peugeot, mais celle devant la maison est une Renault.

9. Le maillot de bain de Martine est bleu, mais celui de Mina est vert.

10. Cette robe est longue mais celle de Mireille est courte.

Exercice 2.20

Bonjour! Je m'appelle Sabine. Quand je dois aller à l'école, c'est à dire le lundi, le mardi, le jeudi et le vendredi, je me lève à sept heures. A la maison, on est cinq. J'ai deux frères et un gros chat qui s'appelle Muesli. J'habite dans une ferme située près de Luçon, en Vendée: le collège n'est pas loin, donc je rentre à midi. Après le déjeuner les classes recommencent à quatorze heures, et je rentre le soir à dix-sept heures. J'ai toujours beaucoup de devoirs à faire le soir, mais avant de me coucher, j'aime lire un roman policier.

Translation:

Hello! My name is Sabine. When I have to go to school, that is to say, Monday, Tuesday, Thursday and Friday, I get up at seven o'clock. There are five of us at home. I have two brothers and a big cat called Muesli. I live on a farm situated near Luçon in the Vendée. The school is not far, so I come home at lunchtime. After lunch lessons start again at 2 pm, and I come home in the evening at 5 pm. I always have lots of prep to do in the evening, but before going to bed I like to read a crime novel.

1.   b

2.   c

3.   c

4.   c

5.   b

Exercice 2.21

Pair work: pupil A writes and reads out (or recites from memory) their daily routine, based on the example by Sabine in **Exercice 2.20**, and should then be able to provide the following information:

1.   what time they get up;

2.   what they have for breakfast;

3.   how they get to school;

4.   what they do when they come home;

5.   how they spend a typical evening at home.

Pupils may ask the further questions given in the Pupils' Book:

6.   what they do to help their parent(s);

7.   what they did yesterday evening;

8.   how much pocket money they received last week;

9.   what they are going to do at the weekend;

10.   what their mobile number is.

They should then note the answers as before.

Exercice 2.22

Dictée

Cette semaine, // nous sommes rentrés // au collège. // Papa aussi // est allé au bureau, // mais maman // est restée à la maison // parce qu'elle avait mal au ventre.

Vive la France!

Les 24 Heures du Mans

(a) One of the best-known car races, the 'Le Mans 24 hours', remains the most demanding. The first '24 hours' took place in 1923; ever since, all the most important makes of automobile have been present every year. The '24 hours' was originally a test-bed for all the technologies that we take for granted on today's cars – safety technology as well as improvements in speed and performance. Even if it seems today as though promoting a make of car is more important than this endurance competition, the 24 hours still represents something unique in the world of motor sport.

It was in 1925 that the famous 'start' – in which drivers have to stand several metres away from their cars to run to them before starting – was born. This lasted until 1969, when it was decided that it was too dangerous.

Le Mans is situated in the north-west of France, on the River Sarthe. The 24 hour circuit is called *Arnage*.

(b) Vrai ou faux?

1. La course des 24 Heures se déroule dans le nord de la France.   Vrai

2. C'est une course facile qui n'est pas dangereuse.   Faux
C'est une course difficile et dangereuse.
It's a difficult and dangerous race.

3. Les 24 Heures ont été importantes pour l'avancement de la technologie automobile.   Vrai

4. On continue aujourd'hui à pratiquer le célèbre départ.   Faux
On ne pratique plus le célèbre départ depuis 1969.
The famous start hasn't been used since 1969.

5. La première course automobile au Mans a eu lieu en 1925.   Faux
La première course automobile au Mans a eu lieu en 1923.
The first Le Mans 24 hour race took place in 1923.

(c) 1. **a**utomobile   A
     2. **r**etroviseur   R
     3. **n**ord   N
     4. **a**ccessoire   A
     5. **g**rand prix   G
     6. **e**xtincteur   E

Arnage: This is the name of the circuit where the 24 hour race is held.

Chapitre 3

A trip around Normandy

Exercice 3.1

Tochiko has never been on a farm. Her family lives in the Vendée, where there are lots of farms, but their house is in La Roche-sur-Yon, a big city, and she wants to go to Normandy to visit a farm where they make cheese! At the end of October, it's All Saints, and she'll have ten days' holiday. Her father is working that week, so her mother suggests spending the holiday with her brothers and sisters on a farm at Pont-l'Evêque, where a famous cheese is produced. She finds an internet site where they promise to find rooms in a 'ferme-auberge' in Normandy. The children are delighted, especially Marie-Christine, who wants to draw animals. It is necessary to find a farm where her wheelchair can get around easily!

After two hours of searching, Tochiko's mother finds the address of an ideal farm where she can rent rooms, of which one will be on the ground floor for Marie-Christine. Fortunately, Mum likes to drive, as Pont-L'Evêque is three hours by road from their home.

Exercice 3.2

1. She lives in a city.

2. She would like to visit one where they make cheese.

3. She will have ten days.

4. Marie-Christine will draw the animals.

5. It is difficult because Marie-Christine has a wheelchair.

Exercice 3.3

1. n'est jamais allée

2. où on fabrique

3. cette semaine-là

4. sa mère lui propose de passer les vacances

5. on promet de trouver

6. elle peut louer

7.   heureusement

8.   à trois heures de route

Exercice 3.4

1.   Je ne suis jamais allé(e) à Paris.

2.   C'est un village où on fabrique du bon pain.

3.   Je suis à Londres cette semaine-là.

4.   Je te propose de jouer au tennis.

5.   Elle promet de venir dîner.

6.   L'ami de ma tante n'est jamais allé au château.

7.   Nous avons vu une ville où on fabrique des violons.

8.   Malheureusement elle est chez elle ce soir-là.

9.   Mon père promet de m'acheter un stylo neuf.

10.   Peux-tu trouver le village?

11.   Ils ne peuvent pas louer le chalet.

12.   C'est dans une ville où on fabrique des automobiles.

13.   La mer est à une heure de route.

14.   Maman me propose de faire de courses!

15.   Mon frère Thomas était en Italie ce jour-là.

Exercice 3.5

1.   J'ai conduit la voiture en Normandie.

2.   Nous avons produit de bons fromages.

3.   Elle a construit une maison en pierre.

4.   Tu as traduit le poème en anglais.

5.   Marcel a traduit l'affiche en français.

6.   Ils ont produit de l'huile d'olives.

7.   Marie-Christine a conduit la voiture de papa.

8.   On n'a pas produit de beurre ici?

9.   Monsieur Moulin a construit la chaumière en 1911.

10.   J'ai traduit les menus pour mon correspondant.

11.   C'est toi qui as conduit la voiture?

12.   Non, je n'ai jamais conduit.

13.   Qui a construit ces maisons?

14.   Il n'a pas très bien traduit – on n'a pas toujours compris!

15.   Dans quelle ville a-t-on produit le Calvados?

Exercice 3.6

1.   Ont-ils terminé leur repas? / Est-ce qu'ils ont terminé leur repas?

2.   A-t-elle choisi une ferme-auberge? / Est-ce qu'elle a choisi une ferme-auberge?

3.   Avons-nous rempli le formulaire? / Est-ce que nous avons rempli le formulaire?

4.   As-tu vendu la maison? / Est-ce que tu as vendu la maison?

5.   Avez-vous vu l'hotel? / Est-ce que vous avez vu l'hôtel?

6.   Nous n'avons pas acheté le bracelet.

7.   Il n'a pas aimé mon dessin.

8.   Elles ne sont pas descendues.

9.   Vous n'êtes pas restés.

10.   Il n'est pas tombé.

11.   Est-ce qu'il a éteint la radio? / A-t-il éteint la radio?
        Il n'a pas éteint la radio.

12. Est-ce qu'elles ont lu le menu? / Ont-elles lu le menu?
     Elles n'ont pas lu le menu.

13. Est-ce que j'ai sorti les poubelles? / Ai-je sorti les poubelles?
     Je n'ai pas sorti les poubelles.

14. Est-ce que vous avez passé l'aspirateur? / Avez-vous passé l'aspirateur?
     Vous n'avez pas passé l'aspirateur.

15. Est-ce que tu es arrivé en retard? / Es-tu arrivé en retard?
     Tu n'es pas arrivé en retard.

Exercice 3.7

Pupils listen to the French dialogue then prepare and present it in front of the class.

The family has arrived in Pont-L'Evêque at lunchtime after a long drive. Everyone is happy at last to be able to get out of the car. Mum drove fast on the motorway, but in town she had difficulty finding the tourist office. On arriving, she was tired.

Mum.	Ouf! These little streets! Where are we?
Tochiko.	Rue Saint-Michel. Hey! There's the tourist office!
Mum.	Do you think we're allowed to park here?
Tochiko.	Sure. Go ahead! *(Tochiko gets out of the car and goes into the tourist office)*
Employee.	Good afternoon!
Tochiko.	Hello, madam. May I have some information on the town?
Employee.	Of course. Here are some leaflets. There's all sorts of information in them. Do you want anything else?
Tochiko.	A street-map of the town, please. How much is it?
Employee.	It's free, miss.
Tochiko.	Thank you, madam. Good bye!
Employee.	Good bye!

Exercice 3.8

1. They arrived in Pont-l'Evêque.

2. They were happy to get out of the car after the long drive.

3. She drove fast on the motorway.

4. It was difficult in town to find the tourist office.

5. She did not have to pay – it was free.

Exercice 3.9

The following is a model answer:

1. Je suis montée dans la voiture et j'ai demandé à ma soeur, «Où est maman?».
Elle a dit «Maman est partie faire un petit tour. Elle est entrée dans l'église, qui
est très belle.» Pascal a éteint son portable. Maman est revenue et elle est
montée dans la voiture. Quand elle a vu le plan, elle était contente.
On a regardé le plan ensemble.

The following is a model answer:

2. Quand nous sommes arrivés, maman a stationné la voiture, sous un bel arbre
qui était très vieux. Tochiko est sortie de l'office de tourisme, où elle a demandé
un plan de la ville.

Exercice 3.10

You are at the tourist office in Pont-L'Evêque. The teacher is the employee.

Pupil	Teacher / employee
1. Est-ce qu'il y a des restaurants?	
	Oui monsieur / mademoiselle. Voici une liste.
2. Merci. Mes amis et moi, on a faim!	
	Il y a un bon bistro ici en face. Préférez-vous la cuisine italienne ou française?
3. Je préfère la cuisine française.	
	Alors, je propose Chez Laura, rue Saint-Michel.
4. Est-ce qu'il faut payer, pour stationner la voiture?	
	Non, c'est dimanche.
5. Demain je vais visiter une ferme.	
	J'espère qu'il va faire beau.

CD
19

Exercice 3.11

They have a chat in the car to decide where to eat. They must find a restaurant quickly, because it is already half-past twelve, and Tochiko's family is quite large. Mum says she went to take a picture of the church and that there was a pizzeria in a little street next to it. Pascal and Mina adore pizzas, but the others choose *Moules Marinière*. Mum eats tagliatelle in wild mushroom sauce and drinks water.

After the meal, everyone gets back in the car and they go to look for the *ferme-auberge*. It's called la Colombière. It's 6 km away from Pont-l'Evêque and is said to be 'easy to see from the road'. Half-an-hour later, Mum turns right and the family finds itself on a long tree-lined avenue at the end of which they finally see the farm.

1.   Il y a une discussion dans la voiture pour décider où manger.

2.   Elle a trouvé la pizzeria en prenant une photo de l'église.

3.   Pascal et Mina aiment les pizzas.

4.   Le déjeuner fini, la famille part chercher la ferme-auberge.

5.   Elle s'appelle «la Colombière».

Je pense que maman a mis une demi-heure à faire six kilomètres, parce que la ferme-auberge était difficile à voir de la route.

Exercice 3.12

1.   Comment vas-tu?

2.   Nous sommes arrivés.

3.   Il fait froid

4.   mais le soleil brille

5.   et je suis contente.

6.   Il y a des animaux

7.   partout.

8.   Peux-tu me téléphoner

9.   jeudi?

10.   Au revoir!

11.   Moi, ça va bien, merci / Je vais bien, merci.

12.   Elles sont arrivées hier.

13.   Il fait assez chaud.

14.   ...mais le soleil ne brille pas maintenant.

15.   Peux-tu me téléphoner samedi de la semaine prochaine?

Exercice 3.13

The text message in 'normal' French:

> Salut! J'espère que tu vas bien.
> Quand es-tu arrivé? Quel temps
> fait-il? J'ai un vélo neuf, c'est génial.
> A demain, d'accord?
> Bisous,
> Marie

Possible reply:

> **Salu – Ça va. Sui arriV**
> **17 h. Ifé tr bo. Ton Vlo é**
> **de kel couleur? @2m1**
> **Cloé – bizz**

The above reply in 'normal' French.

> Salut! Oui, ça va. Je suis arrivée
> à 17h. Il fait très beau. Ton vélo est
> de quelle couleur? A demain,
> Clóe, bisous

Exercice 3.14

Tochiko.	There we are! We've arrived. It's really nice!
Mum.	Oh yes, it was worth coming!
Marie-Christine.	It's brilliant! Toch', help me get out!
Tochiko.	OK, but watch out for the mud!
Marie-Christine.	There's all sorts of animals!
Tochiko.	There are goats, and sheep …
Mum.	Where?
Tochiko.	Over there, beyond the wall, in the field.
Marie-Christine.	How many different animals can you see?
Tochiko.	There's a dog … no, two! I see a cat as well. And some geese.

Mum.	In the stable, there are horses. In the farmyard there are hens with their chicks, and I see two little pigs.
Marie-Christine.	And cows in the fields. Is it a dairy farm here?
Maman.	I don't think so. Maybe the cows belong to the neighbouring farm.
Tochiko.	Here's the lady coming.

1. They think it's really nice.

2. She asks her to help her out of the car.

3. Tochiko tells Marie-Christine to watch out for the mud.

4. The sheep and goats are beyond the wall in the field.

5. They can see hens, chicks and little pigs.

Exercice 3.15

La famille **arrive**. Tochiko **descend,** puis elle **aide** Marie-Christine. Marie-Christine **a** besoin de son fauteuil roulant. Maman le **sort** de la voiture. Pascal ne **fait** pas attention à la boue. Il **court** partout dans la basse-cour. Il **voit** beaucoup d'animaux. Mina **compte** douze animaux différents, dont elle **écrit** les noms dans son carnet. Marie-Christine **est** impatiente de dessiner. Elle **veut** commencer tout de suite, mais la famille **va** faire une promenade avant de prendre un bain et se changer pour le dîner.

arrive	**présent**	**Ier groupe** *(given)*
descend	présent	3e groupe
aide	présent	Ier groupe
a	présent	irrégulier
sort	présent	irrégulier
fait	présent	irrégulier
court	présent	irrégulier
voit	présent	irrégulier
compte	présent	irrégulier
écrit	présent	irrégulier
est	présent	irrégulier
veut	présent	irrégulier
va	présent	irrégulier

Exercice 3.16

1.
arriver

descendre

aider

avoir

sortir

faire

courir

voir

compter

écrire

être

vouloir

aller

2. La famille **est arrivée**. Tochiko **est descendue,** puis elle **a aidé** Marie-Christine. Marie-Christine **a eu** besoin de son fauteuil roulant. Maman l'**a sorti** de la voiture. Pascal n'**a** pas **fait** attention à la boue. Il **a couru** partout dans la basse-cour. Il **a vu** beaucoup d'animaux. Mina **a compté** douze animaux différents, dont elle **a écrit** les noms dans son carnet. Marie-Christine **a été** impatiente de dessiner. Elle **a voulu** commencer tout de suite, mais la famille **est allée** faire une promenade avant de prendre un bain et se changer pour le dîner.

Exercice 3.17

Appartenir, to belong

j'appartiens

tu appartiens

il appartient

elle appartient

nous appartenons

vous appartenez

ils appartiennent

elles appartiennent

Exercice 3.18

Cher Michel,

Nous sommes arrivés à la ferme-auberge en Normandie! C'est génial. Il fait assez beau mais un peu froid. Dans la basse-cour de la ferme il y a beaucoup d'animaux: des cochons, des oies, des poules et des poussins. Comment vas-tu? A bientôt,

Amitiés,

(Mina/Pascal)

Exercice 3.19

Here is an example of what the pupil might write:

Madame,

Je suis très désolé(e): j'ai brisé un vitre dans ma chambre (la chambre bleue). J'ai lancé un livre sur le bord de la fenêtre. J'ai tout remis en ordre. S'il vous plaît, dites-moi combien le vitre va coûter.

De la part de

(...)

Exercice 3.20

This is the story written in the correct order:

1. Hier soir, on a mangé à la ferme.
   En entrée, on nous a proposé un filet de turbot sur un lit d'asperges.
   Le plat principal était du boeuf en croûte avec des carottes.
   Pour nous préparer pour la viande, il y avait un sorbet à la pomme au Calvados.
   Marie-Christine n'aimait pas le sorbet.
   Avant le fromage on a mangé une salade.
   Après l'assortiment de fromages normands on a pu choisir un dessert du buffet.
   Maman a eu du café, mais pas les enfants.

(It may be necessary to explain to pupils that a sorbet is served between courses to clear the palate!)

2. Yesterday evening, we ate at the restaurant.
   As a first course, they offered us fillet of turbot on a bed of asparagus.
   The main course was beef in a pastry casing with carrots.
   To prepare us for the meat, there was an apple and Calvados sorbet.
   Marie-Christine didn't like the sorbet.
   Before the cheese, we had a salad.
   After the assortment of Normandy cheeses we were able to choose a dessert from the buffet.
   Mum had coffee, but the children didn't.

Exercice 3.21

Dictée

Au printemps, // quand il a commencé // à faire beau, // toute la famille // est partie // en vacances. // On est allé(s) à une ferme, // où on a travaillé // avec le fermier // et sa famille.

Vive la France!

The Cave of Lascaux

(a) One of the most remarkable historical sites in the world, the Lascaux Cave is in the Périgord region of France. In archaeological terms, this find is relatively recent. Four teenagers, who were walking in the woods above the Manoir de Lascaux, were the first people for tens of thousands of years, to discover the magnificent paintings in this cave, thanks to the light beam from their torch. It was on Thursday 12th September 1940. The 'gallery' which they had found had opened up after a huge pine tree had fallen.

They didn't know that their discovery would be among the most important archaeological finds of the 20th century.

The paintings mostly represent animals: mainly bulls, but also horses. Away from the light for such a long time, the colours in these paintings have remained remarkably fresh. It's not difficult to visit the Lascaux Cave: it is at Montignac, near the A89 motorway.

(b) Vrai ou faux?
1. La Grotte de Lascaux est un site préhistorique.   Vrai
2. La Grotte a été découverte par des archéologues.   Faux
     La Grotte a été découverte par des adolescents qui se promenaient.
     The cave was discovered by some teenagers walking.
3. La découverte de la grotte remonte au vingtième siècle.   Vrai
4. Quand un arbre est tombé, la grotte s'est ouverte.   Vrai
5. Il y a plus d'êtres humains que d'animaux dans les peintures.   Faux
     Il y a plus d'animaux que d'êtres humains.
     There are more animals than humans.

(c) The following is a model answer.

Salut maman! Ecoute, on se promenait dans le bois et on a trouvé un arbre qui est tombé.

Oui, je crois que c'est à cause du vent que l'arbre est tombé.

Hervé et moi, on a découvert une grotte énorme sous les racines de l'arbre!

Oui! Je crois que la grotte était habitée par des humains! Il y a des dessins sur les murs!

Ne t'inquiète pas. Nous allons revenir tout de suite!

Vocab: a cause de = because of, la racine = root, ne t'inquiete pas = don't worry

Chapitre 4

November in Normandy

Exercice 4.1

On getting back home, Tochiko and her brothers and sisters have got ready to return to school. They enjoyed themselves in Normandy, and made some new friends, including the animals! They learned a lot about life in the country which is the complete opposite to life in the city. They did things they have never had the opportunity to do at home.

Georges and Martine, spent the All Saints holiday at home, but they went out a lot and visited a vineyard in the Loire valley.

All the young people meet up again at school.

Exercice 4.2

Martine.	When did you get back?
Tochiko.	Last night. We arrived late, there was a traffic jam on the motorway.
Martine.	It was an end-of-holiday Sunday evening, it's normal.
Tochiko.	You're right. Thanks for the text messages!
Martine.	And for yours. It's bizarre, mum didn't understand them, it really irritated her!
Tochiko.	What have we got this morning?
Martine.	Hang on. Two hours of maths, then English before lunch.
Tochiko.	That's worked out nicely. I'm really on the ball in arithmetic and our English teacher is going to ask us what we did last week.
Martine.	Yes, but in English …
Tochiko.	No problem. *I went in a farm …*
Martine.	What talent! I'm not very good at English.

1. Tochiko et sa famille sont rentrées dimanche.

2. Un 'bouchon' sur l'autoroute, c'est quand trop de voitures arrivent en même temps.

3. Elle ne les a pas compris parce que la langue des SMS est différente.

4. Elles vont faire de l'anglais avant de manger à midi.

5. Martine pense que le cours va être difficile parce qu'elle n'est pas forte en anglais.

Exercice 4.3

Salut Henri

Je suis **rentré** à la maison. Aujourd'hui, c'est lundi et on est en classe. On est **allés** en Normandie à une ferme. Il y **avait** plein d'animaux. Mon animal **préféré**, c'est le cheval. Il a fait chaud mais il a **plu** tout les jours. Maman et Tochiko **n'étaient** pas **contentes**. Il n' **y** avait pas de télé donc on a dû lire, écrire ou dessiner. On a **fait** des promenades et Marie-Christine **a** dessiné les oies est les **cochons**.

Réponds-moi vite

Pascal

Exercice 4.4

1. Martine a joué au squash.

2. Georges a joué de la clarinette.

3. Ils ont fait du cyclisme.

4. Les enfants sont allés à la pêche.

5. Georges a fait de la natation.

6. Martine a fait de l'escalade.

7. Toute la famille a fait des promenades en forêt.

8. Nous avons joué au tennis de table.

9. La mère de Martine a joué aux échecs avec la propriétaire.

10. Georges et Martine ont joué au badminton.

Exercice 4.5

1. Maman jouait au tennis.

2. Le père de Georges faisait de l'équitation.

3. Mon frère jouait au golf.

4. Quand il était jeune, il faisait de la planche à voile.

5. Georges et Paul faisaient de la voile.

6. Sa mère écoutait la radio.

7. Ma mère faisait du vélo avec papa.

8. La soeur de Paul jouait au foot avec ses amies.

9. Pierre faisait du ski tous les ans.

10. Sophie et Pierre jouaient aux boules au village.

11. Maman ne jouait pas au tennis.

12. Le père de Georges ne faisait pas de l'équitation.

13. Mon frère ne jouait pas au golf.

14. Quand il était jeune, il ne faisait pas de la planche à voile.

15. Georges et Paul ne faisaient pas de la voile.

Exercice 4.6

1. Ma mère jouait au tennis

2. Georges et Martine faisaient du cyclisme.

3. Tochiko a joué au squash hier.

4. Mes frères jouaient au foot.

5. Tu as fait de l'équitation dimanche.

6. Pascal nageait dans la piscine.

7. Pierre a fait du ski l'hiver dernier.

8. Martine a fait de l'escalade jeudi.

9. Les Simonneau jouaient aux boules. / La famille Simmoneau jouait aux boules.

10. Vous vous promeniez.

Exercice 4.7

The following are examples:

1. Ma voiture est bleue; la sienne est rouge.

2. Notre salle à manger est blanche; la tienne est grise.

3. Ton vélo est rapide; le mien roule lentement.

4. Ma guitare est italienne; la tienne est espagnole.

5. Ta mère est généreuse; la mienne aussi!

6. Oral or written exercise.
   Pupils choose objects in the room and compare them with others, in the way shown in **Exercice 4.7**.

Exercice 4.8

Martine, Tochiko and Sabine are chatting in the school playground after lunch.

Martine.	Did you eat well?
Tochiko.	It wasn't bad. My pork chop was a bit hard.
Sabine.	So was mine. It was a bit disgusting. What did you have, Martine?
Martine.	I had a salad. The dressing was tasteless.
Sabine.	Not like the cooking at the farm, eh, Tochiko?
Tochiko.	I tell you, we had some incredible meals, prepared by a real expert …
Martine.	Yes OK. Why don't we talk about something else?
Tochiko.	… every evening, new gastronomic discoveries…
Sabine.	Stop! That's enough! Where are the boys?
Tochiko.	Georges, I don't know. Pascal was playing football just now, on the football pitch.
Sabine.	I saw him this morning. He said that he had made himself some new friends in Normandy.
Tochiko.	There was a family at the auberge with us. Parisians.
Sabine.	I see. Nice?
Tochiko.	Yes. Two brothers. They got on straight away with Pascal.
Sabine.	What did they do?
Tochiko.	Tons of things. They went for long walks, they went mountain-biking in the forest, they went climbing. Me too!

1. She thought it was OK but a little hard.

2. They say things like 'Stop! That's enough' and want to change the subject.

3. She says, 'Every evening, new gastronomic discoveries...'

4. They were playing on the football pitch.

5. He said that he had made new friends in Normandy.

6. He got on well with them straight away.

7. They went on long walks and they went climbing.

Exercice 4.9

1. C'était dégoûtant.

2. Tu as pris quoi?

3. Pas comme la cuisine à la ferme.

4. Bon d'accord.

5. Ça suffit!

6. Si on parlait d'autre chose?

7. Georges, je ne sais pas.

8. Je l'ai vu ce matin.

9. De nouveaux amis.

10. Des tas de choses.

Exercice 4.10

1. C'était délicieux.

2. Tu as bu quoi?

3. Pas comme les promenades à la plage.

4. Si on jouait au tennis?

5. Si on téléphonait à Christine?

6. Si tu achetais ce T-shirt?

7. Vous, je ne sais pas.

8. On l'a vu hier soir.

9. De vieux bâtiments.

10. De grandes voitures.

11. Ce n'était pas difficile.

12. Vous avez vu quoi? / Qu'est-ce que vous avez vu?

13. Si on rentrait à la maison?

14. Il l'a nettoyée ce matin.

15. Des gens importants.

Exercice 4.11

1. I saw them.

2. We watched them.

3. You wrote it.

4. Did you look for it?

5. Mum listened to them.

6. Martine tasted it.

7. I questioned her.

8. You saw me.

9. We packed them away in the cupboard.

10. Dad consulted him.

11. You have eaten them.

12. We met you last week.

13. He called me before lunch.

14. We bought it.

15. Sophie found them.

Exercice 4.12

1. Il l'a trouvée.

2. Elle les a rencontrés

3. Je l'ai vue.

4. Elle l'a lue.

5. Tu l'as écrite.

6. Nous les avons interrogés.

7. Vous nous avez appelés hier.

8. Ils l'ont achetée.

9. Tu les as rangés.

10. Il les a goûtés.

Exercice 4.13

The past participle which has its sound changed by adding –e is: écrit – écrite. In this word, the 't' is sounded because a vowel has been added.

Exercice 4.14

Salut Peter,

Merci pour ta lettre. Je l'ai … **reçue** … mardi matin. Tu m'as demandé de t'envoyer les belles photos de ta maison. Tu les as … **laissées** … sur la commode de ta chambre. Je les ai … **envoyées** … ce matin quand je suis … **allé** … en ville. Maman a cherché ton stylo. Elle l'a … **trouvé** … sous la table. Elle l'a … **donné** … à Martine.

A bientôt,

Amicalement,

Georges

Exercice 4.15

1. The photo that you took is beautiful.

2. The cars that he has driven are French.

3. Thank you for the letter which I received.

4. The buildings which we looked at yesterday are old.

5. Have you read the text message which she received?

6. The chocolates which I sampled are delicious!

7. It was your parents that I saw in the market.

8. The boy she met is very nice.

9. The CDs you bought were expensive!

10. Give me the post-card you have chosen.

Exercice 4.16

1. Les lettres que tu as reçues.

2. Ma mère, qu'il a vue.

3. Les photos que tu as achetées.

4. Les cafés que vous avez aimés.

5. Les filles que tu as appelées.

6. Les patins que tu as portés.

7. La raquette de tennis que tu as essayée.

8. Ta voiture, que j'ai nettoyée.

9. Les SMS que vous avez envoyés.

10. Le menu qu'elle a choisi.

11. Le vélo que tu as emprunté.

12. Les gens que vous avez rencontrés.

13. La chemise qu'il a portée.

14. Le film que nous avons regardé.

15. Le repas que tu as préparé.

Exercice 4.17
Dictée

Mon ami Pierre et sa famille // sont rentrés // hier soir // à la maison. // En arrivant, // ils ont ouvert la porte d'entrée, // ils sont entrés dans le salon, // et sa mère et sa soeur // se sont assises // dans les gros fauteuils.

Exercice 4.18

These are suggested answers.

D'habitude, le soir, je lis des romans policiers, ou je regarde la télé. En vacances, nous allons en France. L'été dernier, par exemple, nous sommes allés en Bretagne. J'ai fait de la planche à voile et j'ai mangé des moules-frites. C'était délicieux.

Exercice 4.19

These are suggested answers.

1. Nous sommes allés au restaurant samedi soir.

2. Ma cousine aime faire de l'escalade.

3. Avec mon père, nous allons à la pêche le dimanche.

4. Je fais du VTT dans la forêt quand il fait beau.

5. Ce matin il y a eu beaucoup de circulation sur le pont.

Exercice 4.20

You have arrived in Paris on holiday. You must write a letter of 90–110 words including something about **four of the following five** points.

An example is given of what might be said for each of the five points, but this would be, of course, to be within a properly drafted letter, and only represents the bare minimum.

1. le voyage;
   Le voyage était très long mais assez confortable.

2. l'hôtel;
   J'ai aimé l'hôtel: il était moderne et il y avait une piscine.

3.   les repas;
     On mangeait bien à l'hôtel. Ce que j'ai aimé le plus, c'était le petit déjeuner.

4.   un nouvel / une nouvelle ami(e);
     J'ai rencontré beaucoup de jeunes français. / Il y avait un garçon qui s'appelle
     Marc qui est très sportif comme moi.

5.   un problème.
     Un jour, nous sommes rentrés à l'hôtel et Papa n'a pas pu trouver la clé.

Exercice 4.21

1.	V	6.	V
2.	V	7.	F
3.	V	8.	V
4.	F	9.	V
5.	F	10.	V

Exercice 4.22

The pupil (on the phone), giving excuses for not being able to meet the person on time, should say:

Je suis désolé(e)!
J'aidais ma mère dans la cuisine.
Je préparais les légumes pour le dîner.
Je me suis coupé(e) le doigt!
Ma mère m'a emmené(e) à l'hôpital.
J'ai quitté l'hôpital à trois heures.

Exercice 4.23

An example is given in the pupils' book of how each pupil should select key words from the columns, to create excuses! If the pupil manages one item from each column, and it makes sense, marks are awarded.

Qui tu es	Où tu es	L'heure	Pourquoi tu es en retard: tu as …
This column shows who they are.	This column shows where they are.	This column shows what time it is.	This column shows their excuse.

The example given:

Allô? C'est **Armand**! Je suis désolé, je suis **à la maison**, il est **midi**. Je ne peux pas venir, j'ai **cassé mes lunettes**!

Vive la France!
The Millau Viaduct

(a) The Millau Viaduct was inaugurated on the 16th December 2004 by President Jacques Chirac. It's the highest viaduct in the world, and it dominates the Tarn valley in the southern part of the Massif Central. Here are some facts and figures:

The highest point of the viaduct is 340 m, as high as the Eiffel Tower. The road bridge is 2.5 km in length, and crosses the valley, linking Clermont-Ferrand to Béziers and Montpellier by the A75 motorway. Before the viaduct was built, motorists had to go through Millau, which nearly always involved lengthy hold-ups. In the construction of the viaduct, 127,000 m³ of concrete, 19,000 tonnes of steel concrete reinforcement and 5,000 tons of steel were used.

And the most interesting fact about this incredible construction? It was an Englishman, Sir Norman Foster and his team, who designed it!

(b) Vrai ou faux?
1. On a construit le Viaduc l'année dernière.   Faux
   On l'a construit en 2004.
   It was built in 2004.
2. Le Viaduc est plus haut que la Tour Eiffel.   Faux
   Il est aussi haut que la Tour Eiffel.
   It is as tall as the Eiffel Tower, not taller.
3. Un pont routier était nécessaire à cause des problèmes   Vrai
   de circulation.
4. C'est un Français qui a fait le dessin finalement adopté.   Faux
   C'était un Anglais
   It was an Englishman.
5. Sur le viaduc il y une route pour les voitures qui fait plus de deux   Vrai
   kilomètres de long.

(c) Pupils are invited to design a poster to attract visitors to the viaduct. There is a tourist centre, car parking, a video lounge where one can learn about the building of the viaduct. There are great views too.

Chapitre 5

Yesterday, today and tomorrow

Exercice 5.1

Georges, Martine, Tochiko, Marie-Christine and Pascal are at the café near the school, the Café des Amis. They are talking about their school day, and their free time. They are talking about what they have done, and what they are going to do. Luckily, access for disabled people is easy. They have to come inside because it is going to rain, and it's already a little cold. The café is packed. The waiter arrives.

Exercice 5.2

Waiter.	Good evening. Are you ready to order?
Marie-Christine.	We haven't quite decided yet!
Waiter.	Shall I come back in two minutes?
Marie-Christine.	No! I think it will be all right. I'm having a coke.
Pascal.	For me, an Orangina.
Georges.	For me too.
Martine.	Me ... er, I'm going to have tea.
Tochiko.	I'd like a strawberry cordial with water.
Waiter.	OK. One coca cola, one Orangina, one strawberry cordial and one tea. Is that right?
Martine.	That's it!
Georges.	What are you going to do this evening, Toch'?
Tochiko.	After dinner I'm probably going to do my homework, then after that, you know, I don't have much time left.
Georges.	I haven't much to do this evening. What do you have, in the way of homework?
Tochiko.	I've got a history essay to do. I'm going to take a couple of hours to finish everything.
Martine.	There's a good documentary on the Romans tonight, on France 2.
Tochiko.	Is there? I love documentaries.
Pascal.	What did you do yesterday, Georges? We didn't see you at the skating rink.
Georges.	I went to the cinema with my parents. We saw a comedy film in English, James Bond stuff. There were subtitles.
Pascal.	What was it like? Did you enjoy it?
Georges.	Yes, it was really funny. Mum loves foreign films.

1. They have to be inside because it is about to rain.

2. They talk about their school day, and what they are going to do this evening.

3. He asks them if they are ready to order.

4. Martine has tea.

5. She is going to do her homework after dinner.

6. On France 2 there is a documentary about the Romans.

7. The previous evening, he was expected to be at the ice rink.

8. He was at the cinema with his parents.

Exercice 5.3

1. Près du collège.

2. Leur journée d'école.

3. Leur temps libre.

4. Les jeunes doivent se mettre à l'intérieur.

5. Il va pleuvoir.

6. Il fait déjà un peu froid.

7. On n'a pas encore décidé.

8. Je reviens?

9. Je crois que ça va aller.

10. Je n'ai pas grand'chose à faire.

11. Qu'est-ce que tu as comme devoirs?

12. On ne t'a pas vu.

13. Il y avait des sous-titres.

14. C'était comment?

15. Tu t'es amusé?

Television in France

Television in France is like everywhere else: a few 'terrestrial' channels, and an astonishing array of satellite and cable channels. In France there are five national channels which you can receive without paying a subscription, and an encrypted channel which necessitates a decoder in order to be received clearly. The five channels are:

TF1   **France 2**   **France 3**   **La Cinq**   **M6**

Arte

La Cinq is a shared channel with **Arte** (pronounced *Arté)*, a German television channel. The encoded channel is called *Canal Plus (Canal +).*

Exercice 5.4

Jean va regarder:

«L'Espion qui m'aimait», puis le Festival de Montpellier.

Claudine va regarder:

«Qui veut gagner des Millions?», puis la Météo, après le Journal.

Justine va regarder:

Le match de basketball, France-Espagne, puis «L'Empire des Dieux»

Jonathan va regarder:

«L'Espion qui m'aimait», puis le Journal.

Marc va regarder:

«L'espion qui m'aimait», puis le Festival de Montpellier.

Exercice 5.5

1. Pupils must write an email of 50–60 words in French to a friend, in which they discuss TV in England and their programme preferences. Here is an example:

    Salut (...)!

    Qu'est-ce que tu aimes regarder à la télévision? En Angleterre il y a cinq chaînes terrestres et des tas de chaînes de satellite. Moi, j'adore le sport. Je préfère regarder Sky Sport mais j'aime aussi les feuilletons comme *Eastenders* et des émissions musicales. Et toi? Quelles sont tes émissions préférées?

    Ecris-moi vite,

    Amitiés, (...)

To show they understand the French instruction to this question, pupils must provide in English:

2. any two examples of British sport programmes;

3. any two adventure films they've seen on TV;

4. two examples of British game shows;

5. two examples of 'soaps' on British TV;

6. two examples of thrillers on British TV.

Exercice 5.6

1. She has finished her homework.

2. She's put away her things.

3. She has put her clothes in the washing machine.

4. She has fed the cat.

5. She has cleaned the bathroom.

6. She is going to take the bins out (later).

7. She is going to arrive at Natalie's in ten minutes.

8. She is going to help Natalie with her maths homework.

9. She is going to watch the weather forecast for the next day on TV.

10. She is going to return for dinner.

11. Je n'ai pas fini mes devoirs.

12. Je n'ai pas rangé mes affaires.

13. Je n'ai pas mis mes vêtements dans le lave-linge.

14. Je n'ai pas donné à manger au chat.

15. Je n'ai pas nettoyé la salle de bains.

16. Je ne vais pas sortir les poubelles.

17. Je ne vais pas arriver chez Natalie dans dix minutes.

18. Je ne vais pas l'aider avec ses devoirs.

19. On ne va pas regarder la météo pour demain.

20. Je ne vais pas rentrer pour dîner.

Exercice 5.7

Quand Martine <u>est sortie</u> elle <u>a vu</u> Georges, qui <u>promenait</u> le chien de son copain. Elle <u>a demandé</u> à Georges si maman <u>était</u> aux magasins. Georges <u>a répondu</u> qu'il ne <u>savait</u> pas mais il <u>a dit</u> qu'il <u>pensait</u> que maman <u>commandait</u> du pain pour dimanche.

Exercice 5.8

1. J'avais trouvé

2. Il avait chanté

3. Elle avait vu.

4. Tu avais mangé.

5. Elle avait rempli.

6. Elles avaient puni.

7. J'avais ouvert.

8. Nous avions joué.

9. Vous aviez voulu.

10. Il avait écrit.

11. J'avais regardé.

12. Vous aviez aimé.

13. Elle avait fini.

14. Nous avions découvert.

15. Ils avaient fait.

Exercice 5.9

1. Martine had sung.

2. Georges had found.

3. The boys had seen.

4. The girls had eaten.

5. She had punished.

6. Dad had read the paper.

7. Mum had written the letter.

8. My sister had opened the parcel.

9. We had wanted to go to Paris.

10. They had built a house.

Exercice 5.10

1. J'étais rentré(e).

2. Il était monté.

3. Elle était descendue.

4. Tu étais entré(e).

5. Elle était née.

6. Elles étaient parties.

7. J'étais arrivé(e).

8. Nous étions sorti(e)s.

9. Vous étiez resté(e)s.

10. Il était tombé.

11. J'étais revenu(e).

12. Vous étiez sorti(e)s.

13. Elle était restée.

14. Nous étions venu(e)s.

15. Ils étaient morts.

Exercice 5.11

1. Michel had come back

2. Patrick and Armand had gone out.

3. The friends had arrived.

4. Philippe's sisters had come down.

5. She had arrived.

6. Dad had gone upstairs.

7. Mum had left.

8. My sister had fallen.

9. We had gone to London.

10. They had come to the reception.

Exercice 5.12

1. Martine n'avait pas chanté.

2. Georges n'avait pas trouvé.

3. Les garçons n'avaient pas vu.

4. Les filles n'avaient pas mangé.

5. Elle n'avait pas puni.

6. Papa n'avait pas lu le journal.

7. Maman n'avait pas écrit la lettre.

8. Ma soeur n'avait pas ouvert le paquet.

9. Nous n'avions pas voulu aller à Paris.

10. Ils n'avaient pas construit de maison.

Exercice 5.13

A day's sailing at Bretignolles-sur-Mer

It was Friday. Dad had promised Martine and Georges that he would take them sailing the next day at Bretignolles, a seaside resort. At Bretignolles, on the Vendée coast, it was possible to hire boats.

On Saturday, therefore, Dad, Georges and Martine left the house after a quick breakfast. On the way, they bought bread, cheese, tomatoes, pears and water to have a picnic at lunchtime. Mum stayed at home, because she suffers from sea-sickness. Martine read in the car. She glanced at the sailing school brochure, in which she discovered that, in order to go onto the sea in a boat with this club, you need to have a licence. It was even forbidden for young people under eighteen to set off without an adult on board. What's more, you had to put on life jackets and even bring emergency flares. She asked Dad if all that was really necessary. He answered that the sea was really dangerous, even if it appeared calm.

On arriving at the club, Dad and the two young people got out of the car and went to look for a dinghy to hire. The weather was perfect. The sea was calm and the sun was shining. Nevertheless, you could see a cloud on the horizon. The instructor came and Dad hired a little boat for four people. They asked him for a deposit of 300 euros! They got into the water, and Dad told the children to push the boat while he unfurled the sail.

1.   He had promisied to take them sailing at Bretignolles-sur-mer.

2.   Mum suffered from sea-sickness.

3.   On the journey, Martine read the brochure from the sailing club.

4.   You need a licence to go out in a boat on the sea.

5.   You must be eighteen to go sailing on your own.

6.   The weather was perfect.

7.   He asked them to push the boat out.

Exercice 5.14

1.	Maman n'aime pas voyager en bateau.	Vrai
2.	Bretignolles est une ville industrielle. C'est une station balnéaire. *It's a seaside resort.*	Faux
3.	Papa, Martine et Georges sont allés faire de la voile le week-end dernier.	Vrai
4.	Papa avait donné la brochure du club de voile à sa fille.	Vrai
5.	Deux personnes de seize ans ont le droit de partir en bateau sur la mer. Il faut avoir dix-huit ans. *You need to be eighteen.*	Faux
6.	Les gilets de sauvetage sont interdits. Les gilets de sauvetage sont obligatoires. *Life jackets are compulsory.*	Faux
7.	On doit respecter la mer.	Vrai
8.	Les dériveurs sont plus gros que les yachts. Les dériveurs sont plus petits que les yachts. *Dinghies are smaller than yachts.*	Faux
9.	Il ne pleuvait pas.	Vrai
10.	Le bateau qu'ils ont loué était prévu pour trois personnes. Le bateau qu'ils ont loué était prévu pour quatre personnes. *The boat which they rented was designed for four people.*	Faux

1.   Mum doesn't like to travel by boat.

3.   Dad, Martine and Georges went sailing last weekend.

4.   Papa had given the sailing club brochure to his daughter.

7.   One must respect the sea.

9.   It wasn't raining.

Exercice 5.15

Pupils will have listed some or all of the words below, and looked them up in the dictionary. Here are the meanings:

du pain	bread
du beurre	butter
du fromage	cheese
du saucisson	salami
du jambon	ham
du poulet	chicken
des fruits de mer	sea food
de la confiture	jam
des frites	chips
des chips	crisps
des pommes	apples
des poires	pears
des oranges	oranges
du chocolat	chocolate
des bananes	bananas
des yaourts	yoghurts
du thon	tuna
des carottes râpées	grated carrots
des salades préparées	prepared salads
de l'eau	water
du coca	coca-cola
du vin	wine
de l'Orangina	Orangina
du lait	milk

Pupils must select seven items to make their ideal picnic, and their partner must guess what they have written.

Exercice 5.16

Dictée

Il y a un café // près de notre école. // On y est allés // l'autre jour // prendre un café // avant de rentrer. // Il faisait très froid, // mais nous nous sommes vite réchauffés // après avoir bu // du chocolat chaud.

Exercice 5.17

Pupils must write a letter in French to a friend, mentioning **four** of the five points listed. Here is a model answer:

Cher Paul / Chère Natalie,

Comment vas-tu? J'espère que tu vas bien. Moi, ça va très bien. L'autre jour, papa nous a emmené(e)s à la plage, où nous avons fait de la planche à voile! Pour moi, c'était la première fois. J'étais très nerveux / nerveuse!

Il faisait assez beau. Le soleil brillait, mais il faisait un peu froid. Géraldine avait le mal de mer. C'était trop amusant!! Moi, j'ai trouvé très difficile de faire de la planche à voile.

Dans la mer, on faisait de la voile aussi, et du ski nautique. C'était dangereux!

A midi, on a fait un pique-nique sur la plage. C'était délicieux. Plus tard, vers quatre heures, nous sommes rentrés à la maison. J'étais fatigué(e), mais content(e).

Ecris-moi vite,

Amitiés,

(...)

Exercice 5.18

On the beach, after the sailing.

Martine.	Thanks Dad, that was brilliant!
Dad.	Wait there. I'll be back!
Martine.	I'm cold.
Georges.	If you had brought your top …
Martine.	I'm going to bring it next time.
Georges.	The sea was lovely. It was quite calm.

Martine.	Yes. I don't like it when it's rough.
Georges.	You were scared.
Martine.	I wasn't! …
Dad.	Here, I've just bought some waffles.
Georges.	Mmm! I love these!
Dad.	Do you want this one or that one?
Georges.	This one, please Dad.
Dad.	Right. This one's for me!
Martine.	What about me?
Dad.	Oh! Did you want one as well? Here …
Martine.	Thank you, Daddy darling!

1. La mer était belle.

2. J'ai froid; tu avais peur.

3. Si tu avais apporté ton pull.

4. Je viens d'acheter des gauffres.

5. Tenez; tiens

6. Translation:

Dad.	Here, I've just bought some waffles.
Georges.	Mmm! I love these!
Dad.	Do you want this one or that one?
Georges.	This one, please Dad.
Dad.	Right. This one's for me!
Martine.	What about me?
Dad	Oh! Did you want one as well? Here …
Martine.	Thank you Daddy darling!

Exercice 5.19

1. **Gentil** (kind) is an adjective. The rest are food nouns.

2. **Cravate** (tie) is an article of clothing. The others are activities.

3. **Rouge** (red) is an adjective. The rest, nouns, are types of building.

4. **Beau** (beautiful) is an adjective. The rest are family member nouns.

5. **Rond** (round) is an adjective. The others (nouns) are landscape features.

Exercice 5.20

1.	**voulait**	**imparfait (vouloir)**
2.	avait acheté	plus-que-parfait (acheter)
3.	étaient	imparfait (être)
4.	jouait	imparfait (jouer)
5.	chantait	imparfait (chanter)
6.	faisaient	imparfait (faire)
7.	venait	imparfait (venir)
8.	avait	imparfait (avoir)
9.	avait remarqué	plus-que-parfait (remarquer)
10.	a pu	passé composé (pouvoir)
11.	était	imparfait (être)
12.	a acheté	passé composé (acheter)
13.	sont revenues	passé composé (revenir)
14.	étaient	imparfait (être)
15.	arrêtaient	imparfait (arrêter)
16.	a aidé	passé composé (aider)

Exercice 5.21

Pupils must design a poster about their favourite group, either on the computer or by hand, showing the details below in French:

The group is giving a concert on

- Saturday 15th July,
- at the Maison Française in Oxford,
- at 19.30.

Admission price is £8.00, but

- under-14s pay only half the normal price, and
- one can buy T-shirts and CDs after the concert.

Vive la France!

The Tour de France

(a) The *Tour de France* takes place every year. It is a cycle race which attracts the most fanatical and determined racers, who are ready to do everything to be able to put on the infamous *yellow jersey*. Whilst it is an annual event, the *Tour* is a unique race. Every year, the route of the *Tour* is different. Small stages of the race outside France have even been added (recently in England!). So how can one compare the exploits of the champions? If you look in the *Tour* archives, you will find that the average speeds of the racers in kilometres per hour have been recorded: in 1903, in the first *Tour*, Maurice Garin managed an average of 25 km/h. The winners of the first five *Tours* were all Frenchmen. More recently, the Spanish have had success with Miguel Indurain; but it is the Americans who have had eight wins (of which seven were by Lance Armstrong) and who currently dominate the sport.

(b) Vrai ou faux?

  1. Le Tour de France a lieu tous les ans.   Vrai
  2. Le parcours de la course cycliste est toujours pareil.   Faux
      Le parcours est toujours différent.
      The route is always different.
  3. Les cyclistes du Tour ne doivent jamais partir de la France.   Faux
      Il y a souvent des étapes hors de la France.
      There are often stages of the race outside France.
  4. Maurice Garin est le dernier gagnant du Tour de France.   Faux.
      Maurice Garin était le premier gagnant de la course.
      Maurice Garin was the first winner of the race.
  5. Les Américains sont très forts en cyclisme en ce moment.   Vrai

(c) Pupils must design a poster announcing the passage of the *Tour de France* through a village in France they imagine that they live in.

Chapitre 6

Peter comes back to France

Exercice 6.1

Peter, Martine's English penfriend, arrived on the 12th December. It was only 5.00 pm, but it was already dark. After a day of wind and rain, it was cold – winter had arrived.

Neither Martine nor Georges had to go to school that day, because it was a Wednesday. So, at 4.30, Mum, Georges and Martine went to fetch Peter at the airport.

Exercice 6.2

Mum.	Hey! There he is! Peter!
Martine.	Oh yes! I recognise him from his photo. We're not allowed to meet the people straight away. They have to wait for their luggage.
Mum.	Shall we have a coffee?
Martine.	If you're paying!
Mum.	OK.

***

Mum.	A large white coffee, please.
Waiter.	And for you sir?
Georges.	A hot chocolate.
Martine.	I'm going to have a tea with milk, like the English!
Mum.	Good idea!

***

Georges.	I see Peter!
Martine.	I see him too! He looks tired.
Mum.	Hello Peter! Have you had a good journey?
Peter.	Hello Mrs Colbert! Not bad, but I had to wait in Customs. I don't like airports! But the aeroplane was comfortable.
Mum.	You ate well, I hope?
Martine.	Oh come on Mum, the journey's too short, you don't have time to eat on the plane!
Maman.	Let's get home quickly then! I've got everything ready, we can eat straight away!
Peter.	Cool! I'm hungry! Where is Mr Colbert?
Georges.	Dad? Still slogging away.
Peter.	Er …?
Martine.	He's at the office, he's working!

1. Peter arrived at 5.00 pm in France.

2. It was cold, after a day of wind and rain.

3. It was dark already.

4. They were not at school because it was Wednesday.

5. Peter had to collect his luggage and pass through Customs.

6. She suggested they have a cup of coffee.

7. She agreed on condition that Mum pay.

8. She had tea with milk in honour of her English penfriend's arrival.

9. He seemed tired.

10. Peter found the aeroplane comfortable.

11. He did not like the airport.

12. He would not have eaten because the flight was so short.

13. Peter expected to see Mr Colbert.

14. Au boulot is an everyday expression for 'at work'.

Exercice 6.3

C'est toujours … **fatigant** … de voyager en avion, parce qu' … **il y a** … trop de monde aux aéroports. L'année … **dernière** …, ma tante canadienne est … **venue** … en Europe avec Doug et Charles, mes … **cousins** … . Pour … **traverser** … l'Atlantique, ils ont … **fait** … un voyage de treize heures. Leur voyage a commencé à quatre heures du … **matin** …! Ils ont passé leur temps à … **attendre** … dans les files d'attente, passer à l'enregistrement, faire contrôler leurs bagages, et ce n'était qu'à dix … **heures** … qu'ils sont finalement … **montés** … par la passerelle pour le vol de Paris.

Exercice 6.4

The following is a suggested answer.

Salut Mimi,

Je suis arrivé(e) à l'aéroport. Il est minuit et je suis très fatigué(e)! Il ne pleut pas mais il fait très froid. Je suis en retard parce que j'ai dû attendre à la douane. Pour passer le temps, j'ai fait des Su-Doku.

Je vais t'appeler demain.

Bisous,

Hélène / Marc

Exercice 6.5

Pupils must play the part of an airport employee, who has to answer passengers' questions.

Here are some suggestions:

1. Excusez-moi, pour aller aux départs, s'il vous plaît?
    C'est tout droit devant vous, juste après le contrôle des passeports.

2. Où sont les toilettes?
    Là-bas, entre le restaurant et la maison de la presse.

3. Pardon, on peut louer des voitures ici?
    Oui, la location de voitures est juste en face de la sortie.

4. Je voudrais acheter un journal. Il y a un marchand de journaux?
    Oui, la maison de la presse est à côté du bureau de renseignements.

5. Où peut-on manger ici?
    Il y a un restaurant et un bar là-bas.

6. Excusez-moi. Où est-ce qu'on peut prendre un car?
    L'arrêt des cars est en face de la sortie, à votre gauche.

7. J'ai envie de boire un café. Il y a un café ici?
    Oui, bien sûr. Il y a un bar à côté du restaurant.

Exercice 6.6

1. Les aéroports sont fatigants mais ils sont nécessaires.

2. Le parking vert est à côté du restaurant Les Alizés.

3. On n'a pas le droit de laisser les bagages non-surveillés.

4. Le vol Paris–Rome était assez court et très confortable.

5. Quand j'arrive en France je téléphone à mes parents.

6. Dans le taxi en route à l'hôtel mon frère a joué avec son PlayStation®.

7. J'ai acheté un magazine que j'ai lu après le dîner.

8. C'était difficile de trouver la consigne.

Exercice 6.7

1. Jean-Paul en a trente.

2. Le chat en mange un(e).

3. On en regarde.

4. J'en ai eu sept la semaine dernière.

5. Tu en veux?

6. Ils en ont dans la cuisine.

7. Il y en a un litre dans le frigo.

8. Pourquoi n'en prends-tu pas?

9. Philippe en a douze.

10. Je n'en ai pas.

11. Elle en a vingt.

12. Il y en a six.

13. On en a deux dans le garage.

14. Ils sont en train d'en regarder un. / Ils en regardent un.

15. J'en ai lu un(e) hier.

Exercice 6.8

After dinner, Peter got settled in at the Colberts' house. He spoke French well for an English boy of his age, but he had forgotten a lot of vocabulary, so Martine took him round the house, reminding him of all the French words for the furniture, the ornaments and the decoration.

First, they went into the kitchen, where Maritne showed him the places laid on the table, that is to say the tablecloth, the knives, the forks, the spoons, the plates and the glasses. She showed him the cupboards and the household machines – the washing machine, the dishwasher and the coffee-grinder. She pointed out the saucepans, the microwave and the gas cooker. There was no carpet on the ground floor, there was tiling on the floor. There was a fridge, and a freezer.

Georges closed the shutters and the windows, and the curtains were drawn. The three young people went upstairs to where the four bedrooms were – the parents' bedroom, those of Martine and Georges, and the guest room, temporarily Peter's bedroom.

In Peter's room there was a bed, with two pillows and a duvet, a chest of drawers, a wardrobe, a small table, a chair, a light and an alarm clock on the bedside table. There was also a small shelf with a few books. In the bathroom, there was the bath, towels, the whole family's toothbrushes, a rug on the floor and a mirror on the wall. Beside the radiator, there was a little bin. The bathroom window looked out onto the courtyard behind the house.

Martine.	Well, the house hasn't changed much, has it, Peter?
Peter.	No. That's true.
Georges.	There are books in your room, if you want to read.
Peter.	Thanks very much.
Georges.	Are you tired, Peter?
Peter.	I'm OK, but I feel that I am going to sleep well!
Martine.	It's already ten o'clock. Do you want to go to bed?
Peter.	Yes I do. What are we going to do tomorrow?
Georges.	Tomorrow we – Georges and I – are going to school. You are going to stay here. You can go for a walk, go for a bike ride …
Peter.	Brilliant. What time do you have breakfast?
Martine.	Seven o'clock, ten past seven … But we have to set off before half-past. You, it's your first day. You get up when you want!
Peter.	Excellent. Right. I'm going to bed. Good night!
Martine.	Good night, Peter. See you tomorrow.

1. They took him round the house because he had forgotten a lot of the French words for household things.

2. They started the tour in the kitchen.

3. It had a tiled floor.

4. They had a coffee-grinder, so they bought coffee beans.

5. The guest room had become Peter's bedroom.

6. In Peter's room there was a bed, with two pillows and a duvet, a chest of drawers, a wardrobe, a small table, a chair, a light and an alarm clock on the bedside table. There was also a small shelf with a few books.

7. He went to bed at ten o'clock.

8. The following day they were at school.

9. They suggested that he go for a walk or a bike ride.

10. She suggested this because it was his first day.

Exercice 6.9

1. Peter ... **est** ... arrivé en France au mois de décembre.

2. Martine ... **a** ... fait la visite de la maison avec Peter.

3. Georges ...**a** ... accompagné les autres.

4. Les enfants ... **sont** ... entrés dans la salle de bains.

5. Martine n'... **a** ... pas parlé anglais à Peter.

6. Pourtant, il ... **a** ... bien compris.

7. Nous ... **avons** ... choisi de bons livres.

8. Vous ... **avez** ... fait un bon voyage?

9. Je me ... **suis** ... amusé dans l'avion.

10. Les amis de Peter l'... **ont** ... emmené à l'aéroport.

11.	Ma soeur ne s'... **est** ... pas couchée tout de suite.

12.	Elle ... **a** ... montré les romans à son ami.

13.	Tu ... **es** ... monté voir la chambre?

14.	Non, je ... **suis** ... resté en bas.

15.	Quand t'... **es** ... -tu levé?

Exercice 6.10

Pupils must ask each other these questions, noting the response of their partner. At the end, they should check to see that they understood their partner correctly. The questions are followed here by suggested ways to begin an answer.

1.	A quelle heure t'es-tu couché(e) hier soir?
	Je me suis couché(e) à ... heures.

2.	A quelle heure te lèves-tu le dimanche matin?
	Le dimanche matin, je me lève à ... heures.

3.	Tu vas à l'école le samedi?
	Oui, le samedi je vais à l'école.
	or:
	Non, le samedi je n'ai pas cours.

4.	Qu'est-ce que tu fais après les classes?
	Je fais mes devoirs ou bien je regarde la télévision.

5.	Comment (par quel moyen de transport) est-ce que tu vas à l'école?
	Je viens à l'école en voiture avec mon père.

Pupils then have to **write** answers to these questions giving true information about themselves.

Exercice 6.11

At ten o'clock in the morning, having got up and had breakfast with Mrs Colbert, Peter borrowed Georges' bicycle and went off for a ride around the area. Before setting off, he examined the bike, and wondered if he knew all the French words for its different parts.

Then he left. He had only travelled two hundred metres when he suddenly stopped.

'How stupid I am!' he said to himself. 'I'm riding on the left, like in England! Here they drive on the right! It's dangerous!' He crossed the road with care, then he got back on the bicycle and went on his way. He went past the church and rediscovered the village shops. Instead of crossing the square, Peter got off the bike and went round the village campsite on foot. He looked at the notices pinned up on the wall of the campsite reception hut. He understood some of them, but not all.

It was cold, but sunny. Despite the cold, you could feel the sun. There was a light dew in the fields, and Peter thought of his friends who were at school. Martine, cheerful, sociable, optimistic, and Georges, headstrong and impulsive but likeable and sincere.

Peter cycled slowly on his way back to the house. He was happy to be in France once again.

Mum.	Hi Peter! So, did you enjoy that?
Peter.	Yes, Mrs Colbert. The countryside is beautiful.
Mum.	I have a surprise for you. On Saturday we're off for a winter sports holiday!
Peter.	Wow! Where are we going to go?
Mum.	The resort is called Les Gets. We're going to rent a ski chalet!
Peter.	Cool!
Mum.	Have you been skiing before?
Peter.	No, never. Where is Les Gets?
Mum.	Look. I've got a map here on the table.

Pupils must write an email in French to a friend, in which they imagine they are Peter and talk about their first day in France at the Colberts' house. They are reminded to mention:

- breakfast
- the bike ride
- the campsite
- the weather
- Mrs Colbert's surprise about the holiday

The email should include, therefore, sentences like these:

- J'ai pris le petit-déjeuner avec Mme Colbert.
- J'ai fait un tour à vélo dans les environs de la maison.
- Je suis allé dans le camping.
- Il fait beau mais froid.
- Quelle surprise! On va partir en vacances de neige!

Exercice 6.12

Mum telephones the chalet rental agency.

The agent.	Good morning! Ski-Famille agency. How can I help you?
Mum.	Good morning, madam. I saw your advertisement on the internet. Are there still chalets available in Les Gets for next week?
The agent.	Yes, madam, I have two left in Les Gets. How many of you are there?
Mum.	Five. Three children, my husband and myself.
The agent.	I have a chalet near the slopes, but you will have to share with another family.
Mum.	Will we be independent?
The agent.	Completely. The apartements are self-contained. You will only share the staircase!
Mum.	Perfect …

Mrs Colbert books the chalet. Then she looks on the internet to find the best way of travelling to Les Gets. By air, it's quite expensive, so she chooses the train.

Exercice 6.13

1. Je partagerai.
2. Il mangera.
3. Elle trouvera.
4. Nous arriverons.
5. Tu choisiras.
6. Vous finirez.
7. Elles rempliront.
8. Je grandirai.
9. Vous attendrez.
10. Nous descendrons.
11. Philippe vendra.
12. On entendra.
13. Elles ne partiront pas.
14. On ne choisira pas.
15. Tu ne regarderas pas.

Exercice 6.14

1. I shall share.

2. He will eat.

3. She will find.

4. We shall arrive.

5. You will choose.

6. You (pl.) will finish.

7. They will fill.

8. I shall grow.

9. You (pl.) will wait.

10. We shall go downstairs / descend / get out of (a car etc.).

11. Philippe will sell.

12. We shall hear.

13. They (f.) will not leave.

14. We shall not choose.

15. You will not look.

Exercice 6.15

1. Elle trouvera.

2. Nous entendrons / On entendra.

3. Tu voyageras.

4. Nous attendrons / On attendra.

5. Vous choisirez.

6. Ils rempliront.

7. Il descendra.

8. Marie arrivera.

9. Je partirai.

10. Tu regarderas.

11. Il nettoiera la voiture.

12. Marc et Philippe quitteront la maison.

13. Georges vendra la bicyclette.

14. Maman mettra la table.

15. Papa passera l'aspirateur.

16. Tu ne mangeras pas le pain.

17. Vous m'attendrez ici.

18. Ils trouveront la carte sur la table.

19. Elle cherchera sur l'internet.

20. Je ne lirai pas le livre.

Exercice 6.16

1.	Futur immédiat	6.	Futur simple
2.	Futur simple	7.	Futur immédiat
3.	Futur simple	8.	Futur simple
4.	Futur immédiat	9.	Futur simple
5.	Futur simple	10.	Futur simple

Exercice 6.17

1. Demain je **vais lire** le journal.

2. Ma mère **écoutera** la radio.

3. Tu **trouveras** la carte sur la table.

4. Vous **allez chercher** sur l'internet.

5. Ma soeur et moi **partirons** vendredi.

6. Georges **ne montera pas** à l'église aujourd'hui.

7. Comment **va-t-il voyager** mercredi prochain?

8. C'est possible qu'il **louera** une voiture.

9. Je **mettrai** ce pain dans mon panier.

10. Quelle pâtisserie **choisirez-vous**?

Exercice 6.18

Dictée

Un de mes camarades de classe // m'a envoyé // une carte postale que j'ai reçue hier. // Il était en vacances // dans les Alpes, // où il faisait du ski // et d'autres sports de neige // avec ses parents // et son petit frère.

Exercice 6.19

1. We shall have.

2. You will go.

3. We shall see.

4. We shall be.

5. They will have to.

6. She will send.

7. I shall be able.

8. You will receive.

9. We shall know.

10. He will hold.

Exercice 6.20

1. Elle viendra.

2. Je courrai.

3. Nous ne saurons pas / On ne saura pas.

4. Elles voudront.

5. Vous verrez.

6. Ils sauront.

7. J'aurai.

8. Tu seras.

9. Monsieur Colbert enverra.

10. Georges et Martine recevront.

11. Saurez-vous?

12. Ils ne courront pas.

13. Elle ne devra pas.

14. Je ne viendrai pas.

15. Verra-t-il?

16. Recevront-elles?

17. Enverrons-nous? / Enverra-t-on?

18. J'achèterai.

19. Elle mènera.

20. Il appellera.

Exercice 6.21

1. passé composé

2. plus-que-parfait

3. imparfait

4. passé composé

5. infinitif

6. présent

7. présent (+infinitif)

8. futur immédiat

9. futur simple

10. futur simple

11. La librairie était fermée.

12. Je suis en train de regarder.

13. J'étais en train de regarder.

14. Je sortirai.

15. Irregular verbs featured in the exercise are: **voir, être, lire, sortir, aller.**

Exercice 6.22

It was Friday evening. All the family was in the process of packing to go off on their skiing holiday in the Alps. Peter came into the sitting room.

Peter.   Excuse me, Mrs Colbert, but …

Mum.   What's the matter, Peter? You are very pale!

Peter.   I do not feel well.

Martine.   Do you have a headache?

Peter.   Yes, and I have a stomach ache.

* * *

Georges.   What are we going to do if Peter can't come on holiday?

Martine.   He must come! We're going to go straight to the duty chemist!

Mum.   OK. Go with Dad in the car. It's quite a long way.

* * *

The pharmacist asked Peter what was wrong, and Peter explained to him that he had a headache and a sore stomach, and that he had slept badly. The pharmacist said that it was nothing very serious, and that he could go skiing. But he advised him to go to bed early and gave him some pills. He said that he was very tired after his school term in England and the trip to France. In the car, Dad teased him.

'So, you don't like skiing, is that it?' Luckily, Peter laughed!

1. Le lendemain.

2. Qu'est-ce que tu as, Peter?

3. Tu as mal à la tête?

4. En train de faire les valises.

5. Je ne me sens pas bien.

6. Qu'est-ce qu'on va faire?

7. Il avait mal dormi.

8. Il lui a conseillé.

9. Papa l'a taquiné.

10. Heureusement.

Exercice 6.23

1. Elle avait mal à la tête.

2. Nous étions en train de partir.

3. Ma mère ne se sent pas bien.

4. Qu'est-ce qu'il va faire?

5. Qu'est-ce que tu vas faire?

6. Ils avaient bien dormi.

7. Je n'avais pas bien dormi.

8. Ils m'ont conseillé.

9. Je leur ai conseillé.

10. Elle m'a taquiné(e).

Exercice 6.24

Pupils create a wordsearch in which all the adverbs on the list in the pupils' book appear, or as many as they can fit in. They can give the wordsearch to another member of the group to do.

Exercice 6.25

Dictée

Après avoir acheté // un médicament, // Peter est sorti // de la pharmacie. // Marie n'est pas sortie; // elle est restée // à l'intérieur.

Vive la France!

Fashion

(a) Paris has always been the European centre for fashion. You only have to think of all the names of the top designers and couturiers to be convinced of it.

Even foreign fashion houses really need to be present at fashion shows which take place in Paris.

Below, a design by Giorgio Armani, who has been one of the 'kings' of fashion for a long time. One also thinks of Coco Chanel, Nina Ricci, Christian Dior and Yves Saint-Laurent. The clothes you see sometimes in fashion shows can be a little strange, but it's here that everyday fashion is born.

(b) Vrai ou faux?

1. Il n'y a pas beaucoup de designers ou couturiers étrangers aussi bien connus que les français.   Vrai

2. A Paris on voit le label des designers étrangers aux défilés de mode.   Vrai

3. Les créations des maisons de mode n'influencent pas les vêtements ordinaires.   Faux
    C'est aux défilés de mode de Paris que naît la mode de tous les jours.
    It is in the fashion shows of Paris that everyday design is born.

4. Giorgio Armani est un des designers les plus importants de Paris.   Vrai

(c) Pupils may create their own fantasy fashion, making a poster labelled in French showing a pair of jeans, a skirt, a top, or a pair of shoes of their own design, with their own 'designer label'.

Chapitre 7

At the ski resort

Exercice 7.1

All the family left the house on Saturday morning at seven o'clock. It was still dark. On the way to the TGV station at Nantes, Peter was able to sleep in the car. Everyone got up very early; no-one had anything to eat. Dad made some coffee and the bags were loaded in the boot of the car.

Setting off, they tried not to make any noise, but it wasn't easy. You could see Mr Simonneau watching the comings and goings from behind his bathroom window. Georges was excited, but Martine was dozing – getting up at such an early hour seemed cruel to her! Mum drove while Dad told her which way to go. There wasn't much traffic. They went along in silence. No-one spoke …

Finding the long-stay car park was easy, and Mum parked the car, after taking a ticket. Dad looked for a trolley for the luggage, and the family headed for the station entrance. Dad spoke to Peter.

Exercice 7.2

Dad.	You see, Peter? It's practical.
Peter.	What is it, Mr Colbert?
Dad.	It's the automatic ticket machine. There are quite a few. Look!
Peter.	Oh yes. How do you …?
Dad.	You only have to touch the screen. You choose your destination … There! Single ticket or return? Then you decide if you want to go first or second class. Go on, touch it! Then, how many are we?
Peter.	Er ... three children and … two adults …
Dad.	Now we wait a few seconds and … there: we have a choice of three TGVs which leave today. And … we'll have to get a connection. That means we'll have to change trains in Paris. Right, half-past eight, 9.42 or 12.20?
Peter.	Eight-thirty?
Dad.	Yes! We will be able to have breakfast on the train. OK! So, I put my credit card in the slot, and ... I enter my PIN. Right. That's done. We can go!
Georges.	Dad, you haven't validated the tickets.
Dad.	You don't have to with tickets from the machines. It's already done!

There were not many people on the train. When it arrived at the *Gare de Montparnasse*, everyone got off and the Colberts and Peter had to cross Paris by tube to get to the *Gare de Lyon*. With the luggage, it wasn't very easy. Martine explained to Peter.

Exercice 7.3

Martine.   First we have to get a 'carnet' – a book of ten tube tickets for the price of six!

Peter.   So it's cheaper!

Martine.   Much cheaper. Also you can use them whenever you need them!

Georges.   But you throw them away afterwards.

Martine.   Yes. We don't recycle them!

1.   The whole family left to go on a winter sports holiday.

2.   There was no conversation in the car.

3.   She thought it was 'cruel'.

4.   He looked for a baggage trolley.

5.   It has a touch-screen system.

6.   It was 12.20.

7.   They would have breakfast on the train.

8.   He thought he had forgotten to validate the tickets.

9.   Tickets from the automatic machines do not need to be validated.

10.   They got there by tube (underground train).

Exercice 7.4

1.   La famille ... **est partie** ... en vacances.   (partir)

2.   On ... **est arrivé** ... à la gare à onze heures.   (arriver)

3.   Vous ... **avez fait** ... un bon voyage?   (faire)

4.   Georges et Martine ... **ont dormi** ... dans la voiture.   (dormir)

5.   Maman ... **a lu** ... la carte routière.   (lire)

6.   Je n'... **ai** ... pas ... **fini** ... de lire le journal.   (finir)

7. Ils ... **ont pris** ... le petit-déjeuner dans le train. (prendre)

8. A Paris ils ... **ont dû** ... prendre le métro. (devoir)

9. Papa ... **a acheté** ... un carnet de tickets. (acheter)

10. Tu n'... **as** ... pas ... **recyclé** ... les tickets. (recycler)

Exercice 7.5

1. Georges n'a pas grimpé dans les arbres.

2. Maman n'avait jamais pris de photos.

3. Jérôme et moi n'avons pas promené le chien.

4. Il n'y avait plus de neige.

5. On ne s'est pas installés sur l'herbe.

6. Tu ne vas plus venir chez nous?

7. M. Colbert n'a jamais voyagé par le train.

8. Martine et ses amies n'ont fait que 30 km à vélo.

9. On ne voit guère de chevaux dans la rue.

10. Paul ne veut pas aller en vacances de neige.

11. Nous n'avons pas ouvert la fenêtre.

12. Tu n'as pas fini ton repas?

13. Ils n'arrivaient jamais à temps.

14. Vous n'allez pas partir dans trois minutes!

15. Personne n'a sorti les poubelles aujourd'hui!

16. Je n'ai rien vu sur le quai de la gare.

17. Mon père ne va jamais trouver son stylo.

18. Je ne monte plus à cheval.

19. Tu n'as pas lu l'article?

20. Mon frère ne joue plus avec le chien de Pierre.

Exercice 7.6

1.   Georges didn't climb the trees.

2.   Mum had never taken any photos.

3.   Jérôme and I did not walk the dog.

4.   There was no more snow.

5.   We didn't sit down on the grass.

6.   Are you not going to come to our house any more?

7.   Mr Colbert has never travelled by train.

8.   Martine and her friends only did 30 km by bicycle.

9.   You hardly ever see horses in the street.

10.   Paul does not want to go on a winter sports holiday.

Exercice 7.7

The Colberts took a whole day to get to their destination. The TGV was fast and comfortable, but they had to change twice. When they arrived in Les Gets, it was already night time, and very cold, but they asked for directions and quickly found the chalet. The chalet owner came to open the door for them. He was called Mr Schmidt. He was chubby and friendly, and had a strong southern French accent.

Dad.	Hello, sir. My name is Colbert.
Mr Schmidt.	Hello everyone.
Dad.	Are you the chalet owner?
Mr Schmidt.	That's right, sir. Carl Schmidt.
Dad.	Let me introduce my family … *(They say hello)* and Peter, our English friend – or rather, my daughter's penfriend.
Peter.	Hello, sir.
Mr Schmidt.	Oh! You can see he already speaks French! Delighted, young man!
Dad.	It's cold! Can we take the luggage up and get settled in?
Mr Schmidt.	But of course, sir. It's this way! It's dark, but I'll turn on the stairwell light. So, you're on the first floor, and you will have all the rooms on this side of the landing. You will share the stairs, that's all.
Mum.	What's the time, Georges?
Georges.	I don't have my watch any more! You remember, I lost it when we went sailing the second time!

Martine.	Daddy, I'm really hungry. Are we eating this evening?
Dad.	Of course! We'll eat at a restaurant. What's the time?
Mum.	Ten past nine! We'd better get a move on! But I want to have a shower and change!
Dad.	Right, that's decided. Georges and I will go and get take-away pizzas. That way you won't have to go out. We can relax and get an early night.
Mum.	You think of everything!
Georges.	And tomorrow we're going to go skiing!

1.   It took all day.

2.   When they arrived it was dark and cold.

3.   The owner, Mr Schmidt let them in to the chalet.

4.   He asks if they can get the luggage in and settle in right away.

5.   He lost it the second time they went sailing.

6.   Martine is so hungry because she has not eaten all day.

7.   It was a bad idea because Mum wanted to have a shower and change and it was too late.

8.   They decided to eat take-away pizzas.

9.   They would be able to get an early night.

10.   She was delighted.

Exercice 7.8

On est arrivés à dix-neuf heures. Il faisait déjà noir, et on voyait des flocons de neige qui tombaient. Mon amie, qui n'avait pas dormi dans la voiture, était très fatiguée. Mon frère lisait la carte, mais c'était difficile et il ne voyait pas très bien. On a dû demander des directions.

Exercice 7.9

1.   Georges is learning to ski.

2.   We are learning to sing.

3.   They are learning to swim.

4.   You learn quickly here: it's a good school.

5.   You (pl.) learn to speak French.

6.   You do not learn.

7.   What are you doing?

8.   I'm learning verbs for tomorrow's test.

9.   They (f.) learn to ice-skate.

10.   He learns his grammar.

Exercice 7.10

1.   Qu'est-ce que tu apprends?

2.   Il apprend à jouer du violon.

3.   Nous apprenons à parler russe.

4.   Pouvez-vous apprendre à la maison?

5.   Il n'apprend pas le français.

6.   Ils doivent apprendre.

7.   Quand apprends-tu à jouer au squash?

8.   Est-ce qu'il apprend à monter à cheval?

9.   Où peut-on apprendre à faire du ski?

10.   Combien de débutants apprennent?

11.   Comment as-tu appris à faire du ski?

12.   Où a-t-elle appris à jouer?

13.   J'ai appris en suisse.

14.   Ils/elles ont appris à danser à Londres.

15.   Je ne veux pas apprendre à nager.

Exercice 7.11

1. La famille est arrivée … **à la** … gare.

2. … **Au** … parking, on a vite trouvé une place.

3. Martine a couru … **à l'**… escalier.

4. On est descendus … **à l'** … arrêt d'autobus.

5. … **A la** … station de métro, on a acheté un carnet.

6. Tu veux aller … **aux** … magasins?

7. Georges est allé … **à la** … banque avec maman.

8. … **A l'** … école, j'apprends à parler anglais.

9. J'aimerais monter … **à la** … Tour Eiffel.

10. Rendez-vous … **à l'** … Arc de Triomphe!

Exercice 7.12

Peter was a beginner, that is to say, it was the first time he was going to go skiing. The morning of his first outing on the slopes, he asked Georges and his parents a lot of questions. At breakfast he was too excited to eat!

The Colberts and Peter went out of the chalet at about nine o'clock in the morning. During the night it had snowed, and everything was covered by a layer of powdery snow. The mountain was even more beautiful than usual, and the snow sparkled in the fir trees. Mum and Dad looked at a little map of the town, and went on foot to the ski shop. Dad hired everything they needed – skis, ski boots and poles, and they bought a ski suit and gloves for Peter who didn't have any. They went back onto the slopes and joined the queue to buy passes for the ski lift. Dad, Mum and Georges set off on red pistes, as they were experienced skiers, while Martine went with Peter to the ski school.

There were three instructors – two men and a woman. Martine explained everything to an instructor who put them in a mixed group of ten beginners.

Exercice 7.13

1. Pierre et Jean les ont mis ensemble.

2. Marie l'a allumée.

3. Je l'ai fait.

4. Ma soeur les a sorties.

5. Tu les as tirés?

6. Papa les a fermés.

7. Ma cousine va la poster.

8. Luc lui a envoyé le paquet.

9. Georges lui a montré son billet.

10. Papa lui a dit bonjour.

Exercice 7.14

1. Plus grande que.

2. Plus petit que.

3. Aussi intelligents que.

4. Plus bavarde que.

5. Plus court que.

6. Plus dangereuse que.

7. Plus bas que.

8. Plus glissants que.

9. Moins utiles que.

10. Aussi pratique que.

Exercice 7.15

1. Peter est plus grand que Georges.

2. Georges est aussi grand que sa soeur.

3. Les garçons sont plus gentils que les filles.

4. Elle est plus bavarde que Paul.

5. Mon oncle est plus petit que ta tante.

6. Les skis sont plus dangereux que les vélos.

7. La rivière est plus basse que la ville.

8. La rue est plus glissante que le trottoir.

9. Les trains sont moins confortables que les voitures.

10. Oui, mais ils sont plus pratiques.

Exercice 7.16

1.	George court <u>vite</u>.	George runs quickly.
2.	Sabine mange <u>lentement</u>.	Sabine eats slowly.
3.	J'aime lire <u>rapidement</u>.	I like to read fast.
4.	Ma soeur écrit <u>bien</u>.	My sister writes well.
5.	Marcel mange <u>peu</u>.	Marcel eats little.
6.	Ses amis nagent <u>beaucoup</u>.	His (Her) friends swim a lot.
7.	Tu lis <u>vite</u>.	You read quickly.
8.	Marie vient <u>souvent</u> chez nous.	Marie often comes to our house.
9.	L'oncle de Georges fume <u>trop</u>.	Georges's uncle smokes too much.
10.	J'ai conduit <u>dangereusement</u>.	I drove dangerously.

Exercice 7.17

Les adjectifs	*Les adverbes:*
faible	bien
long	vite
rapide	longtemps
lent	rapidement
petit	lentement
mal	trop
bon	souvent
mauvais	peu
actuel	beaucoup
	actuellement
	bientôt

Exercice 7.18

1. Jacob court moins vite que moi.

2. Vous êtes plus intelligentes qu'Anne.

3. Philippe écrit aussi rapidement que Jeanne.

4. Notre voiture est plus confortable que la tienne.

5. La porte s'ouvre plus facilement que la fenêtre.

6. Ton T-shirt est plus beau que le mien.

7. La maman de Jacques n'est pas aussi belle que la nôtre.

8. Le stylo de Paul marche mieux que le mien.

9. Ta maison est plus moderne que la leur.

10. J'attends moins longtemps ici qu' à l'autre arrêt de bus.

Exercice 7.19

Peter was very interested in the differences between the ski resort and the Vendée village, and also between France and England, his native country. He spoke about it with Georges and Martine. Where he lives, near London in England, there are lots of people and traffic, and it is dangerous to play in the street.

Peter.	There are more tourists here than in the Vendée!
Georges.	Yes. That's normal. In winter, they have already been gone for some time.
Martine.	On the other hand, they come here to go skiing, so there are lots of them.
Georges.	What are the differences between Les Gets, and the town where you live in England?
Peter.	Well for a start you don't see any houses like these ones.
Martine.	Of course. You only see chalets where there's lots of snow in winter.
Peter.	Yes. The chalet roofs are bigger than the roofs of English houses. Also, the streets are wider. There's less snow in England. Sometimes, in winter, it doesn't snow at all.
Georges.	Are there other differences?
Peter.	Sure. Where I live, the buildings are taller. There are more cars in the streets. It's hard crossing the road. The suburban area is huge. Here, there's the village, and outside the village there's the countryside – lots of green spaces where there are no houses.
Martine.	That's true. There are farms, and that's all. Here, we're in the mountains, there are also hills. In the Vendée, near the Atlantic coast, the land is flat. Here it's noisier, but it's nice!
Georges.	I would like to come to England. Your country is obviously very different from France. Will you invite me, Peter?
Peter.	Of course!

Exercice 7.20

1. Peter was interested in the differences between the Vendée village and the ski resort, but also the differences between France and England.

2. It would have been dangerous to play in the street.

3. In the Vendée there were no tourists left; here there were more than ever.

4. The houses are completely different.

5. The ski resort streets are wider and there are fewer cars than in England.

6. He says there is sometimes no snow in England

7. The Alps are mountainous and the Vendée is flat.

Exercice 7.21

1. Il en a parlé

2. Il y a beaucoup d'habitants.

3. C'est dangereux de jouer.

4. Plus de touristes.

5. Donc ils sont nombreux.

6. La ville où tu habites.

7. Des maisons comme celles-ci.

8. Seulement là où il y a beaucoup de neige.

9. Ici, on est à la montagne.

10. J'aimerais venir en Angleterre.

Exercice 7.22

1. Elle en a chanté

2. Il n'y avait pas vraiment beaucoup d'habitants.

3. C'était facile de voir.

4. Moins de visiteurs.

5. Ils ne sont pas très nombreux.

6. La salle où vous mangez.

7. Des jours comme ceux-ci.

8. Seulement là où il y a moins de circulation.

9. Là, on est dans les collines.

10. J'aimerais quitter Londres.

Exercice 7.23

1. Cette pièce-ci est plus grande que celle-là.

2. Cette maison-là est meilleure que celle-ci.

3. Cette fille-ci est plus grande que celle-là.

4. Celle-ci est plus jolie que celle-là.

5. Celui-là est plus petit (or court) que celui-ci.

6. Ces voitures-ci sont plus rapides que celles-là.

7. Ces disques-là sont plus légers que ceux-ci.

8. Cet ordinateur-ci est plus lourd que celui-là.

9. Ces chiens-ci sont plus aimables que ceux-là.

10. Ces stylos-là écrivent mieux que ceux-ci.

Exercice 7.24

1. Elle chanterait.

2. On mangerait.

3. Je trouverais.

4. Tu arriverais.

5. Vous choisiriez.

6. Je finirais.

7. Elle remplirait.

8. Nous grandirions.

9. Vous vendriez.

10. Il descendrait.

11. On vendrait.

12. Tu entendrais.

13. Philippe ne sortirait pas.

14. Maman ne punirait pas.

15. Vous ne regarderiez pas.

Exercice 7.25

1. Il regarderait.
2. J'entendrais.
3. Vous voyageriez.
4. Elles iraient.
5. Vous puniriez.
6. Ils rempliraient.
7. Nous mangerions.
8. Papa partirait.
9. Je sortirais.
10. Tu trouverais.

11. Il nettoierait la maison
12. Maman et Papa quitteraient la maison.
13. Martine achèterait la bicyclette.
14. Maman sortirait les poubelles.
15. Papa arriverait tôt.
16. Tu ne mangerais pas le poisson.
17. Vous m'écouteriez.
18. Ils demanderaient un dépliant.
19. Elle courrait au magasin.
20. Je ne verrais pas l'émission.

Exercice 7.26

Dictée

Ma copine m'a téléphoné(e). // Elle m'a posé beaucoup de questions // sur les devoirs d'anglais // que nous voulions faire ensemble. // Elle m'a demandé de venir chez elle, // mais je n'ai pas voulu // y aller // car j'étais trop fatigué(e).

Vive la France!
Louis Blériot

(a) Louis Blériot is best known for having crossed the Channel by aeroplane. He was a French engineer whose profession was the construction of car headlights. But aviation fascinated him, and he built his own aircraft in 1907. Blériot received the first ever pilot's licence in 1910. When the *Daily Mail* challenged aviators to be the first one to cross the Channel, Blériot did not hesitate in accepting the challenge, and took off from Calais early in the morning of 25th July 1909 in another aircraft of his own design. He arrived safe and sound in Dover thirty-seven minutes later, which is more or less the time it takes to cross the Channel through the Tunnel today! Blériot duly received the 25 000 Francs (500 €) offered for a successful undertaking of this exploit. Born in Cambrai (northern France) in 1872, Blériot died after a heart attack in August 1936.

(b) Vrai ou faux?

1. Louis Blériot a traversé la Manche en avion avant la première guerre mondiale.   Vrai

2. La profession de Louis Blériot était: pilote de l'air.   Faux
   Louis Blériot était ingénieur.
   Louis Blériot was an engineer.

3. C'est Blériot qui a construit l'avion avec lequel il a traversé la Manche.   Vrai

4. Blériot a gagné le prix offert par un journal anglais.   Vrai

5. Blériot avait soixante-quatre ans quand il est mort.   Vrai

(c) Pupils must create a wordsearch puzzle using these words:
INGENIEUR
BLERIOT
PILOTE
AVION
AVIATEUR
LANTERNE
TRAVERSER
MANCHE
BREVET
DEFI

... and give it to others to solve!